THE IRWIN SERIES IN ACCOUNTING

Consulting Editor

WILLARD J. GRAHAM, Ph.D., C.P.A.

University of North Carolina

BOOKS IN THE IRWIN SERIES IN ACCOUNTING

Holmes, Maynard, Edwards, and Meier
ELEMENTARY ACCOUNTING
INTERMEDIATE ACCOUNTING

Holmes and Meier
ADVANCED ACCOUNTING

Neuner
COST ACCOUNTING: Principles and Practice

Holmes
AUDITING: Principles and Procedure
BASIC AUDITING PRINCIPLES

Holmes and Moore
AUDIT PRACTICE CASE

Kennedy and McMullen
FINANCIAL STATEMENTS

Anderson and Schmidt
PRACTICAL CONTROLLERSHIP

Hill and Gordon
ACCOUNTING: A MANAGEMENT APPROACH

Mikesell and Hay
GOVERNMENTAL ACCOUNTING

Schmidt and Bergstrom
FUNDAMENTAL ACCOUNTING

Meigs
PRINCIPLES OF AUDITING

Grinaker and Seiler
AUDIT PRACTICE CASE

Pyle and White
FUNDAMENTAL ACCOUNTING PRINCIPLES

Anthony
MANAGEMENT ACCOUNTING: Text and Cases

Shillinglaw
COST ACCOUNTING: ANALYSIS AND CONTROL

Moore and Stettler
ACCOUNTING SYSTEMS FOR MANAGEMENT CONTROL

Murphy
AUDITING AND THEORY: A CPA REVIEW

Ladd
CONTEMPORARY CORPORATE ACCOUNTING
AND THE PUBLIC

Contemporary
Corporate Accounting
and
the Public

CONTEMPORARY CORPORATE ACCOUNTING AND THE PUBLIC

By DWIGHT R. LADD, D.B.A.

Professor of Business Administration
University of Western Ontario

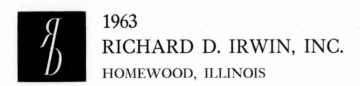

1963

RICHARD D. IRWIN, INC.

HOMEWOOD, ILLINOIS

First Printing, August, 1963

Library of Congress Catalog Card No. 63-19882

For Betty

and for Bob, Kathy, and John

FOREWORD

This book rests upon two propositions. The first is that the large modern corporation has become a major repository of economic and social power—power which must be used in the interests of society. Thus it is of utmost importance to society that it know and understand the extent and the uses of this power. (I do not suggest that this power has been gathered in the corporation by intent or design; indeed its existence is perhaps not always recognized by those who hold it.)

The second proposition is that accounting is a principal means (which is not to say sole means) of communication about the affairs of corporations to those outside the corporations who are concerned with these affairs. Thus accounting has the vital social role of passing on to the public, information about the extent and uses of corporate powers.

The purpose of the book is implicit in these propositions. It is an examination of the extent to which the conventions and procedures of contemporary accounting are compatible with its vital social role. Its basic concerns are first, with the question, "Why account?" and flowing from that with the question, "What to account for?" Concern with "How to account?" is essentially incidental. Any human activity seems to require an occasional reconsideration of its *raison d'être*, for we seem able to make regular adjustments in procedural details without seriously reviewing the broad objectives which underlie the procedures. Because of the great changes in the nature and the role of the corporations being accounted for, I believe that accounting has a great need for such a reappraisal now.

In the discussions which follow, I will recommend certain changes in definitions, conventions, and procedures, and I wish to acknowledge that some of these may be beyond the limits of practicability *at the present time*. However, I think this is less a matter of technology than of attitude. Our ability to answer difficult questions and to solve difficult problems has been increasing and continues to increase at a phenomenal pace. The basic constraint here is in our ability to ask questions and to state problems. I will suggest here some different approaches to accounting for large corporations which will require information not now readily available. I believe, however, that if the questions are asked it is highly likely that they can be answered. Furthermore, I believe that asking the questions is the important thing.

Accounting is a completely derived art and what it does and how it does it must be derived from the needs of those at either end of the chain of accountability. These needs have been and are changing with astonishing rapidity; accounting has not. Whether accounting makes the specific changes in concepts and procedures recommended here is of less importance than that it change. What follows is given in the interests of the greater flexibility needed to meet rapid economic and social change. It is not my desire to substitute new dogma for old.

*   *   *   *   *

My wife has sometimes wondered aloud about the amount of time which professors spend in talking—especially when the talking carries on past the normal dinner hour. Well, one thing that we sometimes achieve by our talks is to stimulate the writing of books, and this book is the result, above all else, of talking with a great many people about the problems of the social role of large corporations and of accounting for them. (I do not imply that the book will stand as ultimate justification of professional talking.) Consequently, it is appropriate that I acknowledge that in preparing this book, I have been helped by virtually everyone with whom I have talked about these matters. My debt is on a grand scale and much is owed to many who will disagree with much that I have written.

A very special acknowledgement must be made to several hundred students who have sat in my classes over the several years during which my ideas have been forming. They have always been a very effective sounding board for these ideas, and on the whole, I think, a patient one. Their forthright criticism of my ideas and careful propounding of rebuttals have both contributed much to this book.

Beyond all these, there are persons whose willingness to criticize has been the source of great help and whose readiness to encourage, the source of much satisfaction. From my father-in-law, Royal C. Nemiah, has come constant intellectual stimulation which I acknowledge with affection. Officially he is a Professor of Greek, but in the tradition of great teachers, he has always taught students rather than subjects. Though by marriage rather than by matriculation, I have long been one of his students and in many discussions about our society and the role of business in it, he has helped me shape many of my ideas—quite often by disagreeing with me.

Professor Ross Graham Walker, of the Harvard Business School, my friend and teacher for over fifteen years, has examined parts of the manuscript and once again has given me the benefit of his tremendous insights into all matters relating to business. Mr. W. H. Ferry, of the Center for the Study of Democratic Institutions, encouraged me to proceed with this writing when it was little more than a half-formed idea and was quick to encourage again when, as it must, the going became rough. My colleagues, Professors John T. Nicholson and C. Kennedy May at the University of Western Ontario, and Mr. John H. McArthur at IMEDE in Lausanne, Switzerland, have given me more time and attention over many questions and problems than I have deserved. Indeed, Professor Nicholson, in spite of writing problems of his own, has at times, been indispensible to me. The detailed criticisms of Professor Willard J. Graham of the University of North Carolina have been of immeasurable help—especially in connection with Chapters Seven and Eight. My secretary, Mrs. Clara Black, has with hard work and uncommon patience, typed and retyped and relieved me of many chores of manuscript preparation.

How bachelors write books, I do not know. Without my wife's readiness to make things easy for me in the many little ways that wives know about and above all, without her unfailing understanding of when I needed to be encouraged and when I needed to be pushed, this book would never have been written.

In spite of all this help, the pleasure of writing has, happily, been mine alone, as must be the responsibility for what has been written.

DWIGHT R. LADD

1962
LONDON, CANADA

TABLE OF CONTENTS

CHAPTER   PAGE

One. INTRODUCTION 1
THE PLAN OF THE BOOK.

Two. THE CORPORATION, ITS REPONSIBILITIES, AND
ACCOUNTING 9

Three. CORPORATION OBJECTIVES AND ACCOUNTING 18

Four. COMPARABILITY IN CORPORATION REPORTS 25
Uniformity in Accounting Procedure.
Changing Price Levels. Summary.

Five. THE PROCEDURAL BASES OF ACCOUNTING 38
Consistency. Materiality. Money. Permanence. Income
Taxation. Past and Future.

Six. VALUE AND CAPITAL 50
Monetary. Purchasing Power. Productive Capacity.

Seven. INVENTORY ACCOUNTING 63
Specific Identification. First-In, First-Out. Average Cost.
Last-In, First-Out. LIFO and Income Taxation.

Eight. ACCOUNTING FOR FIXED ASSETS 77
Replacement Cost. Decline in Value. Depreciation Accounting.
DEFERRED TAXES. ACCOUNTING FOR LEASED FIXED ASSETS: The
Accounting Problems. ACCOUNTING FOR NATURAL RESOURCES.
Summary.

Nine. COMPLEX BUSINESS COMBINATIONS 106
Holding-company Statements. Conditions for Consolidation.
Accounting for Mergers. Pooling of Interests.

Ten. COMPENSATION 123
ACCOUNTING FOR PENSION PLANS: Basic Characteristics. The Ac-
counting Problems. STOCK OPTIONS: Characteristics of Stock
Options. Definition of Cost. Determination of Cost. Grant Date.
Date Exercised. Annual Deductions. Market Value. Disclosure.

Eleven. INTANGIBLE RESOURCES 142
CONTEMPORARY ACCOUNTING PROCEDURES: Resource Valuation.
Income Determination. THE RATIONALE OF ACCOUNTING PRO-
CEDURES: Discrimination.

Twelve. RESPONSIBILITY FOR ACCOUNTING: A SUMMING UP .. 158
Authority of Management.

INDEX 171

Chapter One

INTRODUCTION

I

It was probably about 5,000 years ago in some dusty town in the Tigris-Euphrates valley that a merchant or a land speculator first undertook to use in his business the resources of someone not directly involved in that business. At such a moment, when an outsider first acquired an interest in a business and the business first accepted a responsibility to the outsider, accounting must have begun. When the outsider entrusted responsibility for some of his resources and some of his welfare to the business with which he was not directly involved, a need arose for information about how the responsibility was being met. This provision of information about the status and progress of a business to properly interested outsiders has, from that day to this, been a primary function of accounting.

As the nature of business and its relationship with outsiders has changed and evolved, accounting has had to change and evolve in order to continue to meet its responsibility for providing those who have a proper interest in a business with reliable and adequate information about the business. Particularly as the responsibilities of the business become more widespread and as the business becomes more remote from those to whom it is responsible, the greater the need becomes for information on which to base evaluations. Furthermore, such changes require constant consideration of the extent to which changes in the conceptual and procedural bases for preparing and disseminating information are necessary.

1

It can be said with assurance that accounting does change constantly. However, it can also be said that changes which have taken place have, to a large extent, been introspective in the sense that they have resulted from reappraisals of how certain accepted objectives could best be met rather than from questioning the relevance of the objectives themselves. Accounting has not kept pace with the marked changes which have taken place during the past quarter century or so in the role of business— especially large corporations, the concern of this book—in our society. What A. A. Berle, Jr., has called The Twentieth Century Capitalist Revolution[1] has resulted in a new orientation of business responsibilities and new concepts of appropriate business activities and objectives. It seems clear, for example, that satisfaction of the stockholder interest in corporations is no longer the sole or even the primary responsibility of corporation managers; yet to a considerable extent accounting concepts and procedures are firmly based on the premise of the paramountcy of the ownership interest. It is perhaps not so clear, but it surely can be argued, that corporations have turned toward maintenance of competitive position, growth, and "good citizenship" and away from maximum profit as their major objective; yet accounting is tightly tied to the assumption that maximum profit, achieved in an essentially short run, is the primary objective of the corporation. These and other responsibilities and objectives of contemporary large corporations provide both the starting point and the continuing background for this discussion of the present-day practice of accounting.

---

[1]Professor A. A. Berle, Jr., whom I have never met, has some responsibility for this book since his many writings on the subject have, for a number of years, kept me thinking about these matters. Among his books on this subject are: *The Modern Corporation and Private Property* (with Gardiner C. Means) (New York: Macmillan Co., 1932); *The Twentieth Century Capitalist Revolution* (New York: Harcourt, Brace, 1954); *Economic Power and the Free Society* (Santa Barbara, Calif.: Center for the Study of Democratic Institutions, 1957). In addition Professor Berle has contributed the preface to a most timely and important symposium, *The Corporation in Modern Society*, E. S. Mason, ed. (Cambridge, Mass.: Harvard University Press, 1960).

II

In America the corporation has developed as the principal instrument for the utilization of human, material, and monetary resources in the production and distribution of goods and services and for rewarding those who provide these resources. Since ours is a society overwhelmingly concerned with the production and distribution of goods and services it is not surprising that the corporation has become the very center of our social and economic existence.

The corporation is, in law, the "person" who owns or controls and uses the resources and rewards those who provide them, and thus it is common to speak of corporate activities, of corporate responsibilities, of accounting for the corporations. In fact, it is the managers and directors of the corporation ("the management group") who make the decisions and direct the activities of the corporation, who hold, in the short run, the powers of the corporation. Furthermore, since these men for the most part provide for their own succession, they actually hold the powers of the corporation indefinitely. Consequently it would be most appropriate to speak of management activities, of management responsibilities, of accounting for management. However, managers always act in the name of and on behalf of the corporations: they represent the corporation, but it never represents them. Furthermore, the corporation (General Motors, U. S. Steel, AT&T, etc.) rather than the men who manage it, is what most of us readily comprehend. Consequently, the phrase "accounting for corporations" will generally be used here, even though it is recognized that it is ultimately the actions of the management group which are being accounted for.

III

Essentially this book is concerned with two questions. To what extent should corporations inform properly interested persons outside the management group about their affairs? What should be the conceptual and procedural bases for passing on such information? While the corporate image makers have

3

lately involved themselves with these matters, such communications remain in large part the special function of accounting. Therefore, this is a book about accounting, though it is not concerned with the procedures and conventions of bookkeeping and statement preparation nor with the collection and processing of accounting data. The reader is assumed to have a working knowledge of the basic ideas and procedures of accounting but not the expertise of the trained accountant. Nor is this book an attempt to provide that expertise. No "answers" to the technical problems which are daily faced by the practicing accountant or the student will be found here. Indeed, some questions are raised without answers attempted because this book is only incidentally concerned with "how to account." Its concern is with "why account" and, flowing from that, "what to account for."

The general structure and certain specific applications of contemporary accounting theory and practice have been considered in terms of a specific view of the broad economic and social role and objectives of the corporations being accounted for. This view of corporate role and objectives, described in the following chapter, and the accounting requirements which flow from them is central to all that follows. Indeed, much of what is said here will have only limited relevance to another view of the role of the corporation and of accounting for it. This coverage of specific problem areas is not exhaustive but represents a personal and arbitrary selection. Nonetheless, the topics discussed are quite representative and are, by any standard, of first-rank importance.

At the risk of irritating the professional who may come upon this book, technical language and jargon are avoided as far as possible as are those operational matters and relatively minor points which so fascinate the expert. Given the great influence of corporations in our society, the need for information about their activities and the ability to understand the significance of that information are of concern to all intelligent citizens. The problem is of too great importance to permit it to remain obscured by the niceties of discussion among experts.

IV

THE PLAN OF THE BOOK

A consideration of the two questions posed above requires some prior discussion of who are "properly interested outsiders," of corporate responsibilities to those outsiders, and of the nature of corporate "affairs." The following chapter includes a review of some current thinking about the role and responsibilities of the modern corporation and the requirements for some degree of broad social control which flow both from the great power implicit in that role and from the great scope of these responsibilities. The chapter also includes a brief sketch of the role of accounting in such a control mechanism.

In Chapter Three the apparent shift in corporation objectives from profit maximization to maintenance of competitive position, growth, and "good citizenship" is discussed and the implications of this shift for accounting are considered. Accounting is the principal instrument for communication between the corporation and its constituencies and the way the instrument is used must conform to the relationship between and activities of those at either end of the channel of communication.

If accounting is to communicate about corporate affairs with any effectiveness there must be some degree of uniformity and comparability among corporation reports. At the present time, much of the usefulness of corporation reports is destroyed by lack of uniformity in accounting methods, by failure to indicate methods used, and by failure to make explicit provision for changing monetary values. The arguments for and against uniform methods and price-level adjustments are reviewed in Chapter Four.

Accounting is a system of measurement as well as a means of communication, and thus any discussion of accounting must concern what is being measured and measurement procedures. These latter are the subject of Chapter Five in which the basic conventions which underlie all accounting measurements and communications are reviewed. It is almost universally agreed that accounting is concerned with measuring the amounts of and changes in corporate capital, but there is considerably less agreement about the precise nature of corporate capital. The definition of corporate capital is the subject of Chapter Six.

The balance of the book, excepting the last chapter, is concerned with several specific problem areas in which the concepts and procedures discussed in the preceding chapters are of particular importance. The extreme changes in the value of money in the past twenty years and the apparent changes in the basic objectives of the corporations have created particular difficulties in accounting for resources held by corporations over considerable periods of time, among which inventories and plant and equipment are the most prominent. The several aspects of accounting for these resources are discussed in Chapters Seven and Eight respectively. Accounting for inventories has been further complicated by "direct costing," a technique developed in response to the need for more sophisticated data for internal decision making. In the case of plant and equipment, a relatively new difficulty resulting from the increasing tendency to lease rather than to purchase is also discussed. The chapter also includes a discussion of accounting for so-called wasting resources.

Chapter Nine is concerned with the ever-increasing scope of corporations' activities and their increasing tendency to cut across traditional industry boundaries. Automobile companies manufacture locomotives and waffle irons. Chemical companies manufacture ethical drugs. An abrasives and adhesives company makes recording and reproducing equipment. Virtually all manufacturing companies are involved in making missiles or other military equipment for the armed forces. Because of its concentration on the interests of ownership and the stockholder, accounting has not developed procedures for reporting adequately on these widespread and frequently unrelated activities of corporations. Simultaneously, it is often desirable to ignore in accounting the economic artificialities created by forms of organization which result in the parts of an essentially integrated whole being legally separated into discrete units.

Two somewhat related accoutrements of the present-day corporation—pensions and stock options—have given rise to important accounting problems which have not yet been resolved but whose resolution is of extreme importance in terms of the use of accounting reports as a means for broad evaluation of corporations' performance. These are the subjects of Chapter Ten.

Chapter Eleven is concerned with intangible resources in general and in particular with such things as advertising and promotion and research and development—things which seem in large part a function of the shift to maintenance of competitive position and growth as the foremost corporation objectives. To date accounting has failed to recognize the tremendously increased magnitude of these elements of corporations' activity compared with their scope fifteen or even ten years ago. These are, nonetheless, the areas of corporations' activity where the public interest and concern are most apparent and direct, and therefore accounting for them must be improved.

Finally, in Chapter Twelve, the process of developing and instituting changes in accounting concepts and procedures is considered. It will be suggested that many of the problems discussed previously result from the fact that there is no clearly defined locus of responsibility for developing accounting concepts and practices, nor is there any recognized authority for enforcing discipline within that heterogeneous group of people in business, government, and education which makes up what is loosely called the accounting profession. To a very great degree, accounting is largely controlled by the very people whose activities are being accounted for.

V

The foregoing are, in outline, the specific topics which will be discussed in this book. The list is not claimed to be comprehensive, but most of the major problems of contemporary accounting are considered. Furthermore, the coverage need only be broad enough to demonstrate the gap which exists between the needs of society for information about our large corporations and the quantity and quality of information being provided by contemporary accounting. This book is concerned with creating an awareness of that gap and with contributing to its being narrowed. Changes suggested in connection with the problems discussed here are, in general terms, applicable to other problems.

Chapter Two

THE CORPORATION, ITS RESPONSIBILITIES, AND ACCOUNTING

I

Accounting in all its scope is concerned with all business large and small and with many nonbusiness organizations. This book is concerned only with accounting for "big business" because the great need of the community for information (and thus for accounting) is created by the very bigness of big business. Whether one takes *Fortune's* "Five Hundred" or the "Two Hundred" of Berle and Means or another of several such reckonings[1] it is certain that a relatively small group of large or otherwise important corporations dominate our economy in the broadest sense, and in diverse other ways exert a profound influence on the lives of us all. Indeed it seems clear that these corporations have become second only to government (and perhaps equal with government) as the major locus of power, employed or latent, in our society. Furthermore, one must be aware of the possibility that the military arm of the government and the military supply section of business may together be our major power center. (We were forcefully reminded of this possibility and the dangers inherent in it by former President Eisenhower in his last address before leaving office; an address which

---

[1]An up-to-date summary of the concentration of business power is contained in Carl Kaysen, "The Corporation: How Much Power? What Scope?" E. S. Mason (ed.), *The Corporation in Modern Society* (Cambridge, Mass.: Harvard University Press, 1960), Chap. 5.

may well have been his most important, though largely neg-lected, public utterance.) At any place and at any time there is an obvious need for accounting for such concentrations of power in the interests of the preservation of freedom. Beyond this general case two specific conditions, arising from our own place and time, make essential the availability of information about the status and affairs of these corporations.

The first of these conditions relates to our struggle with the Soviet Union and its allies—both the obvious and direct conflict in such places as Berlin and Viet Nam and the competition to gain the adherence of the new and underdeveloped nations. In this struggle the conduct of American business and its personnel is, willy-nilly, a major factor. Trade among nations in the products of business is a crucial element. Both these facts make business an instrument of national policy, and if the instrument is to be used effectively in the national interest the nation must know what it is doing.

The second condition may be called the cybernetic revolu-tion which is well on its way to taking over from the capitalist revolution. That the work of industry—indeed, the direction of much of that work—will increasingly be done by machines is no longer a matter for speculation. We are now realizing some of the implications of this revolution[2], and there is no doubt that both during the transition to automated industry and after, con-trol of business—the agency through which this revolution is being carried out—is required by the public interest.

It is neither assumed nor desired that we will abandon our system of private direction of enterprise in favor of a state-directed system. In our present setup, the power of decision rests in the hands of the managers of corporations except in areas specifically circumscribed by law or custom, and this seems unlikely to change in the foreseeable future. Given the fact that these corporations have enormous power in our society, there must be a basis for a review of decisions even though the power of decision remains within the corporation. It is a major func-

---

[2]See, for example, W. H. Ferry, *Caught on the Horn of Plenty* (Santa Barbara, Calif.: Center for the Study of Democratic Institutions, 1962).

tion of accounting to provide the information on which to base such reviews.[3]

II

An important task of accounting is to provide to properly concerned persons outside the management group information about the status and probable progress of the corporation. It is typically contended that this task involves making "an independent appraisal of the fairness of reported results of managements' stewardship as shown in annual financial statements made available to shareholders. Fairly stated financial statements result not only from dependable recording and summarization of financial transactions, but also from proper application of generally accepted principles of accounting."[4]

This view of the role of accounting well fits that part of our tradition which holds that corporation managements are ultimately responsible to the owners of the corporation—the stockholder. Some corporate annual reports still use the second person, reciting to the stockholder the achievements of "your company," "your management," "your factories." The ritual of the annual stockholders' meeting, complete with box lunches and Lewis D. Gilbert, is the symbol of this tradition. On a more important level, one finds that much of the theory of investment within the individual business is firmly anchored to this tradition.

For some time, however, there have been many indications that the tradition is no longer a relevant description of corporate responsibilities (if, indeed, it ever was). Probably starting in 1932 with Berle and Means's *The Modern Corporation and Private Property*, there has been an ever-increasing articulation

---

[3]If it is true that we are to fight a long "war" with the Soviet Union, utilizing economic rather than military weapons, we may well be forced into increased state direction of enterprise for businesses may be our principal "fighting" organizations in such a war. It is, after all, a long time since Western nations have looked to private enterprise to organize and direct their military forces, and the ineffectiveness of such private-enterprise armies (as in Nationalist China) against state-directed forces is apparent.

[4]N. J. Lenhart and P. L. Defliese, *Montgomery's Auditing* (8th ed.; New York: Ronald Press, 1957).

of the view that corporate responsibility is far more widespread. Many proponents of these views have been corporation managers themselves; the idea of broad corporate responsibilities is not exclusively the idea of critics of the corporation. This broad view of the corporation's responsibility is well summarized in this statement (typical of many) of the late Louis D. Brown, one-time chairman of the Johns-Manville Corporation:

In the evaluation of a complex industrial society the social re-sponsibility of management has broadened correspondingly. Manage-ment no longer represents, as it once did, merely the *single* interests of ownership; it increasingly functions on the basis of a trusteeship which endeavours to maintain, between the four basic interlocking groups, a proper balance of equity. Today the executive head of every business is accountable not only to his stockholders but to members of his working organization, to his customers, and to the public.[5]

Taken literally, the foregoing suggests for the corporation a most awesome social role. The maintenance of "a proper balance of equity" among virtually all elements of society would seem to require the assumption by corporations of much of the traditional roles of government, of educational institutions, of the church. The parallel with feudalism is remarkably close for that system was characterized by the acceptance by the *seigneur* of the obligation to maintain a balance of equity among the elements of the society. Apparently, no one has yet sug-gested that the several corporate constituencies should give fealty to the corporation executive as the constituencies of the seigneury gave fealty to the seigneur, but this seems a not-illogi-cal extension of the idea expressed above.

Even if taken less literally, Mr. Brown's statement indicates very clearly the downgrading of the stockholder interest in corporations which has taken place. It is not now, if it ever was, the paramount interest, but is at best coequal with the interests of a whole congeries of constituencies or publics. Corporation managements are responsible to many besides the stockholders,

---

[5]Quoted by Howard R. Bowen in *Social Responsibilities of the Business-man* (New York: Harper, 1953).

12

and therefore accounting reports on the "results of management's stewardship" should be conceived of as far more than reports to shareholders alone.

Before leaving the question of responsibility it is important to recognize that there is surely one more than the "four basic interlocking groups" Louis Brown recognizes. Management itself is an important part of the corporate complex, with rights, desires, aspirations, and its own needs for equity. Managers would not be human if, in their attempts to reconcile the interests of the other constituencies of the corporation, they did not, implicitly at least, consider their own interests. The tradition that management is accounting for itself to shareholders puts management in the unsatisfactory position of passing judgment on its own definition of its own interests and on the way it has satisfied those interests. The position of contemporary management needs to be given legitimacy.

Virtually all segments of the community, including corporation managers, have come to have important interests in the status and progress of the large corporation, which is by way of saying that the corporation has important responsibilities to all of them. These responsibilities are a function of the corporation's role as our principal instrument for the utilization of human, material, and monetary resources in the production and distribution of goods and services, and for rewarding those who provide these goods and services. Since the supply of virtually all these resources is less than the demand for them over the long run, it is in the interest of the community—and thus a responsibility of the corporation—that they be used efficiently and rationed according to need. Since the rewards are generally made from the same stock of resources, it is in the community interest and a responsibility of the corporation that the rewards be equitable and be socially and economically efficient.

All of the following discussions of accounting concepts and procedures are based on the foregoing definition of the corporation's responsibility, and it is assumed that this responsibility is owed to several constituencies—stockholders, management, workers, customers, suppliers, and the public.

III

Any system of responsibility involves a degree of control over those who are responsible by those to whom they are responsible. A control system may be incredibly complex, but it will always include three basic elments: a *standard* of performance for the controlled organization, a mechanism through which the controller receives necessary *information* about the performance of the organization, and a process by which the controller can *command* the organization to adjust its performance. This book is specifically concerned with the second of these elements—information. The nature of the command mechanism is beyond its scope although, in passing, it appeared during such events of recent history as the steel-price affair and the drug-inspection law that ready access to the several media of publicity can be extremely efficacious command mechanisms. Objective or standard of performance can be readily defined as safeguarding the public interest, though this definition probably raises more questions than it answers since the nature of the public interest will depend upon specific conditions at specific times. For purposes of these discussions, "the public interest" has been defined in terms of the efficient and equitable use of the resources the corporation controls.

Whether more formal standards and command mechanisms are one day instituted or whether we rely on informal, *ad hoc* agencies, the control process will essentially rest upon the ability of those outside the management group to ask informed and intelligent questions and to suggest change and improvement where the answers indicate the need. The crucial element in this process is the basis for asking questions: complete and reliable information about the corporation's progress, status, and plans. That the information needed goes beyond the financial information which is the particular province of accounting is obvious. Nevertheless, a very great deal of what corporations do and do not do is expressed in financial terms and financial data make up the important nucleus of needed information.

The basis of the corporation's responsibility as it has been defined here (and indeed, the basis of the powers of the corporation) is its control of resources. Consequently, control over the way in which the power is used and the responsibilities are met begins with the possession and evaluation of information about these resources by those affected by their use. In general terms, this process of evaluation involves answering two sets of questions. The first and most important set concerns the present and the future.

1. What resources does the corporation control and what obligations has it incurred in obtaining control of them?
2. What is the value of these resources?
3. What are the commitments or plans for the use of these resources in the future?
4. What is expected to result from these planned uses?

The second set of questions is of secondary importance, relating as it does to the past.

5. What resources did the corporation acquire since the last accounting?
6. Where did these resources come from?
7. What were the results achieved by the use of the resources on hand at the last accounting?

Much of the remainder of this book is a discussion of the extent and the relevance of the information generally available for answering these several questions. At this point, however, certain general prescriptions for such information can be stated. In the first place, the information must be related to the present and to the future, not to the past. Once a decision has been made and resources committed, congratulation or recrimination —depending upon the outcome of the act—are about the only possible courses of action. While it is far, far easier, in general, to hold post-mortems than it is to make prognoses, the only real value of the post-mortem is that it may lead to better prognoses in the future by indicating errors in past ones. The important task—and often an incredibly difficult one—is to analyze the probable results of contemplated future actions. Until a decision is actually implemented it is always possible to change plans and accept the opportunity of using resources elsewhere.

In the second place, information must be basically complete. Ideally, all the resources in the possession of or under the control of the corporation must be known, and all the commitments of resources must be known. What can, in fact, be known will be limited by inevitable uncertainty about the future and by the availability of time and money for obtaining information. The position of one attempting to evaluate the use of resources by a corporation without complete information is rather like that of the ship's navigator who is unaware of the unseen portion of the iceberg his ship is approaching.

Finally, the information must be understandable. Obviously the facts surrounding the control and use of a wide range of resources by corporations are not simple and understanding them requires a degree of knowledge and effort on the part of the reader or listener. This requirement, however, should not be a convenient excuse for confused terminology and for failure to explain adequately how certain important figures were determined. And since the information is used in the evaluation of many corporations, being understandable requires a suitable degree of comparability or uniformity among the statements and reports of all corporations.

In summary, the information required to effectively evaluate corporations must be as complete as possible. It must be relevant to the future, within the limits of tolerable uncertainty, and it must be understandable and comparable.

At the present time, the persons, organizations, concepts, and procedures which together comprise what is usually called financial accounting are the principal mechanism by which this sort of information about corporations is made available. In general, the information currently available from this source is almost exclusively concerned with the past; it is rarely complete and is neither sufficiently understandable nor comparable. However, this does not mean there is need for a new mechanism, if for no other reason than that the pool of highly skilled and devoted personnel and a host of important and effective processes and relationships are virtually irreplaceable. Basically, the only requirement is for a redefinition of purpose, a rededication to the well-established maxim of accounting that the uses to which information is to be put should govern both the conceptual and procedural bases on which the information is prepared and disseminated. In the past quarter century, the over-riding responsibility of our large corporations has become not to stockholders alone but to a whole congeries of constituencies which is, in fact, our society. Thus accounting information is, or should be, used by the community at large, but because accounting has not recognized this, the information is frequently not relevant to these uses.

Chapter Three

CORPORATION OBJECTIVES AND ACCOUNTING

For many years now, accountants have given the bulk of their attention to the measurement of annual income. Professor Moonitz, in the first Accounting Research Study, refers to the "central position that income determination has and does occupy in accounting." Concepts of income have been much debated and the ultimate criterion in evaluating proposed changes or new developments in accounting procedures has been "effect upon income." Corporate net-income figures are widely publicized and all sorts of judgments about dividends, stock prices, wages, prices, contributions, management efficiency, and so on are based upon them.

Since accounting is presumably derived from the activities and needs of those at either end of the chain of accountability and since accounting places so much emphasis on measuring and reporting annual net income one might reasonably conclude that the achievement of maximum annual net income is the principal objective of corporation managers. Further, one could conclude that those to whom the managers are responsible are primarily concerned with management's effectiveness in achieving maximum annual income. Actually, there are many indications that corporate survival and growth (in the long run the two are the same) are the principal objectives of contemporary corporations and that these objectives are implicitly accepted by most of those to whom the corporations are responsible.

The mystique of unlimited potential which characterized

America through the nineteenth century and the first two decades of the twentieth seemed virtually obliterated by the depression psychosis, to use Professor Galbraith's words, which was the legacy of the early 1930's. During the late 1950's and the 1960's, however, the possibility and desirability of growth seemed restored to its former position as one of the major articles of the American faith—especially so since the Russians began to publicize their own growth. The debate about desirable rates of economic growth and how to obtain them filled a major place in the 1960 presidential campaign. A recent study of the causes of growth in companies states in its introduction:

> Granted that a successful business future comes neither automatically nor easily, is its provision chiefly a laudable management maxim, or really a practical primary responsibility? Compounding the magnitude of the assignment is the nearly universal desire for something considerably better than mere corporate perpetuation— a task difficult in a rapidly changing business world.
>
> The demands for "growth" are incessant. And the label "growth firm" has become increasingly synonymous with success, seemingly replacing "blue chip" as the corporate status symbol of the nineteen sixties.[1]

The desire for growth may, of course, be nothing more than an essentially defensive reaction to an ever-increasing population with the resultant ever-increasing work force. Surely the continued development and expansion of so-called automation spur growth and attempts to grow, because in a great many cases automation is practical in only fairly large units. (Automation, as it displaces workers, also adds to the available work force.) The increasing mechanization of data processing together with developments in communications generally have fostered growth by increasing the capacity of individual managers to manage. Data for decision making are available in time periods whose brevity was undreamed of twenty years ago, and analyses of problems may now be made with levels of sophistication barely contemplated until very recently.

---

[1] Robert B. Young, "Keys to Corporate Growth," *Harvard Business Review*, Vol. 39, No. 60 (Nov.-Dec., 1961).

In addition to all these essentially external forces which tend to make growth a desirable objective, some other forces work directly on the businessman himself. Professor Galbraith has written vividly of the important relationship of power to size in our society.[2] If a society gives its accolades to the "biggest" it is not surprising that members of the society will strive to become the biggest. As has been suggested many times, the high top rates of personal-income taxation tend to restrict severely the accumulation of wealth, and thus growth of his enterprise may be the only symbol of achievement available to the manager.

The reasons behind the emergence of growth as a principal corporation objective no doubt include all of the above and many more. No doubt a certain amount of simply running in order to stand still is also involved. One might suggest that a significant portion of the effort in such industries as soap and tobacco results not in growth of those industries or of the companies in them but results rather in keeping any one company from being squeezed out. Whatever the reasons for it, the increased emphasis on growth seems to have relegated profit maximization out of its primary position in the hierarchy of corporate goals.[3] For a very long time (certainly since Adam Smith) it was accepted dogma that businessmen made their decisions with an eye to maximizing profits. Businessmen do try to earn profits, but the idea of a reasonable profit seems to have displaced to some extent the concept of maximized profits. We are told, for example, that "one of the important tasks of Sears' territorial vice-presidents, in fact, is to be certain that their

---

[2] J. K. Galbraith, *American Capitalism: The Concept of Countervailing Power* (rev. ed., Boston: Houghton-Mifflin Co., 1956), chap. III.

[3] One has the impression that professors and researchers in business administration have, in large numbers, recognized that profit maximization is no longer the primary objective of corporations. (cf. R. N. Anthony, "The Trouble with Profit Maximization," *Harvard Business Review*, Vol. 38, No. 6 [Nov.-Dec. 1960]. Economists seem to have continued to cling to the profit-maximization asssumption to a far greater extent, though not all economists have done so (cf. J. K. Galbraith, *op. cit.*, and W. J. Baumol, *Business Behaviour, Value and Growth*, [New York: Macmillan Co., 1959]).

local managers do not maximize profits."[4] The growth study referred to earlier suggests:

Few businessmen would argue with the simple statement that the primary aim of a business in a free enterprise economy is to make a profit. But this implies not only a profit today, but also continued profits tomorrow. For a company is only "successful" if it is laying the framework for a continuously profitable future, as well as producing a satisfactory profit today.[5]

One reason for a diminishing emphasis on maximum profit is not hard to find for it is surely related to the declining influence of the shareholder. (There may be a question of which is cause and which is effect here, but it does not seem significant.) By tradition, by usage, indeed by law, profits belong to the stockholders. That is to say that while profits may be retained for use in the business without the specific approval of the stockholders, the only other use to which they may be put is disbursement to stockholders. In many European countries management is entitled to a tantième or bonus specified by law as a certain percentage of profits, but in general bonuses must be paid to our manager before profit is calculated. They are an expense of the business. As long as the stockholder was supreme, there was strong argument for operating the business in a way which would maximize "his" profits and the amounts which could be disbursed to him. Once the stockholder was relegated to a status which is, at best, coequal with virtually everyone else in the community, it became rather pointless to continue striving to accumulate that which only he could have.

The tendency away from maximum profit as an objective, then, is closely related to the acceptance of the idea of widespread corporate responsibilities and the simultaneous rejection of responsibility to stockholders alone. There is an abundance of examples of corporate activities which have only the most tenuous connection (if any connection at all) with profit maximiza-

---

[4]Herryman Maurer, *Great Enterprises* (New York: Macmillan Co., 1959), p. 113.
[5]*Environmental Change and Corporate Strategy* (Menlo Park, Calif.: Stanford Research Institute, 1960), p. 4.

tion. The steady and increasing flow of corporate philanthropy generally and support of higher education in particular seem unlikely to maximize profits—especially when the money supports poets and philosophers. (Nor is it related to the traditional "best interests of the stockholder," for there may still be Harvard men among the ranks of shareholders who are quite adamant about not wanting any of "their" money to go to Yale.)

Many construction decisions involve aesthetic considerations which give an opportunity to add to the luster of corporate good citizenship but almost surely do not maximize profits. One may commend Seagrams for creating a work of art while erecting an office building, rather than adding to our oversupply of unimaginative, uninspired glass and stainless-steel cubes. At the same time, one may wonder whether Seagrams will sell enough additional whiskey to those aesthetically pleased by the building to offset its cost.

The railroads gave up millions of dollars in profits by their failure to attempt to liquidate money-losing passenger services in the late 1940's and early 1950's. Regulatory commissions, of course, frequently prevented liquidation, but the companies often did not initiate action, and among the reasons for this was the obligation they felt to the communities served.[6]

It will be pointed out by some that a fairly high rate of corporate-income taxation encourages philanthropy, expensive art in banking rooms, and the like since, in general, these are tax-deductible expenses. Uncle Sam, it is suggested, pays 50 per cent of the cost. So he does, but it is equally true that the remaining 50 per cent is at the expense of the stockholders. High rates of income taxation may have encouraged the drift away from profit maximization but they do not explain it.

The apparent displacement of profit maximization by maintenance of competitive position and growth as the major objective of corporation managers—a phenomenon with far-reaching implications in itself—is of first-rank importance in any

---

[6]Dwight R. Ladd, *Cost Data for the Management of Railroad Passenger Service* (Boston: Division of Research, Harvard Business School, 1957), chap. III.

consideration of contemporary accounting. If maintenance of position and growth is the primary objective of corporations and if this is generally accepted as a proper and just goal, corporate performance needs to be appraised on this basis. Accounting should be providing those to whom the corporations are responsible with information on which to base such appraisal. To an unfortunate degree, contemporary accounting provides the form but not the substance of this information.

The successful maintenance of position or achievement of growth over a period of time is manifested by a comparison of resources held at the beginning and end of that period of time. Have a corporation's aggregate resources or stock of capital increased or diminished or stayed the same over a period of time? To what extent are any changes the result of either new capital received from or distributed to persons outside the corporation on the one hand, or directly from the production and distribution of goods and services? Answers to these questions are the most direct indications of whether management has, in fact, maintained the corporation's position or achieved growth or caused decline.

The balance sheet and the funds statement are the principal sources of such information. The balance sheet is a dual description of the corporation's capital at any particular point in time, with the sources of the capital (creditors, stockholders, profitable operations, etc.) and the uses to which the capital is being put (cash, inventories, plant, etc.) the two elements of the description. The funds statement is a description of the changes which have taken place during a period of time in these sources and uses of capital, indicating changes resulting from operations, from new resources brought into the corporation, from withdrawal of resources from the corporation, and from shifting of resources within the corporation.

The balance sheet has always been a part of corporate financial reports. The funds statement is a much more recent addition to these reports and is not yet universally included. (One hopes for universal acceptance of the recommendations contained in a recent AICPA research report[7] which would give the funds statement a status in corporation reports in all ways equal to that of the balance sheet and income statement.)

Unfortunately, the typical balance sheet (and the funds statement derived from it) does not give the sort of information it should. Because of the conventional bases for the valuation of resources and capital, the statements do not generally indicate current resource and capital values. Thus they do not make possible measurements of growth. The basis for resource and capital valuations is the subject of a subsequent chapter. For the moment it can be said that the single-minded attention to income measurement has resulted in the balance sheet being little more than a residual. LIFO inventory valuation, for example, may result in a more reasonable measure of current income (see Chapter Seven) but it results in values for inventories which bear virtually no relation to the actual current value of the goods themselves. The significant understatement of the value of various production and distribution facilities held under lease which results from current procedures for accounting for these leases is often excused or condoned on the grounds that the measurement of income is not distorted by these accounting procedures (see Chapter Eight). Other similar situations are discussed in subsequent chapters. Taken together they indicate the extent to which accounting seems to have ignored the shift in corporate objectives from maximizing net income to the maintenance of position and growth. It is not the intention here to suggest that net income is unimportant and that accounting should ignore it. However, statements of current resource values and explanations of changes in these values are most pertinent to appraisals of the extent to which a goal of maintaining position and growing has been met. Consequently, accounting should devote far more of its attention to these measures and should cease regarding them as simply residuals of the process of annual income determination.

---

[7] Perry Mason, *"Cash Flow" and The Funds Statement* (Accounting Research Study No. 2) (New York: American Institute of CPA's, 1961).

Chapter Four

COMPARABILITY IN CORPORATION REPORTS

To those who have understood the processes of accounting, it has always been known that two qualified accountants could each calculate the profit of the same business for the same period of time or calculate the value of any of the resources of that business and, in either case, could arrive at significantly different amounts. It must hastily be added that in doing so the accountants would act with equal skill, with complete honesty, and would always utilize only recognized and accepted accounting procedures. Corporation reports can be prepared in diverse ways and quite typically are.

Those who understand accounting also know that accountants have gone through the past fifteen or so years of constantly changing monetary value assuming that, like Gertrude Stein's rose, a dollar is a dollar is a dollar. Accounting is possibly the only system of measurement which has accepted the Herculean task of trying to make measurements with a constantly changing measuring stick.

Essentially free choice from among a too-wide range of measurement criteria and the use of an unpredictably variable measuring stick have had the predictable result: there may be little comparability among the reports of several corporations— even of those in the same industry—and, as a result, the usefulness of these reports in evaluating the performance of the corporations is severely restricted.

Uniformity in Accounting Procedure

It is to the credit of the accounting profession that it has not attempted to obscure the permissiveness of its procedures; indeed, members of the profession have publicized it quite regularly. In 1957, in a speech subsequently given wide circulation, Marquis Eaton, then president of the American Institute of Certified Public Accountants, stated "that two otherwise identical corporations might report net income differing by millions of dollars simply because they followed different accounting methods—and that the financial statements of both companies might still be . . . in accordance with generally accepted accounting principles."[1] Reasons for this situation are not hard to find for there are acceptable alternative procedures for virtually every accounting problem. The most significant of these problems are probably inventories, depreciation of plant and equipment, and so-called intangibles, all of which are discussed in some detail in later chapters.

This situation can be briefly illustrated by considering the accounting for a business' $1000 investment in a new piece of equipment estimated to have a useful life of twenty years. Under the current practice of income determination it is necessary to deduct the $1000 against the gross revenue of the succeeding twenty years "in a systematic and rational manner."[2] This seems a relatively simple and straightforward matter until one turns to a standard work such as *Depreciation* by Grant and Norton and finds at least ten rational and systematic manners from which to choose. The amount of depreciation expense to be deducted from gross revenues in the first year of the life of this equipment could be $125, $100, $75, $50, $25, as well as an unpredictable amount related to use of the equipment.[3] All other things remaining the same, the company's profits could vary

---

[1] From an address by Marquis G. Eaton delivered before the Illinois Society of Certified Public Accountants, June 7, 1957.

[2] American Institute of Certified Public Accountants, *Accounting Terminology Bulletin Number 1* (New York, 1961), paragraph 56.

[3] E. L. Grant and P. T. Norton, Jr., *Depreciation* (New York: Ronald Press, 1949), chap. 10.

by these amounts and the net book value of the particular equipment would range from $975 to $875 after one year. Where millions of dollars of plant and equipment are involved these differences would themselves be in the millions.

This situation creates two major problems for anyone attempting to use accounting statements and reports to evaluate corporations' performance. The first of these problems, already referred to, is that it can make comparisons among even relatively similar companies quite meaningless. It is true that intercompany comparisons are of limited value at best, because even similar companies may, at any particular time, be subject to quite different conditions. However, comparisons can give rough indications of relative performance and suggest the extent to which a corporation is carrying out its avowed responsibilities. It is, therefore, important that these comparisons not be vitiated by the use of completely different accounting procedures.

In the second place, and in terms of a single company, historical analysis of the company's statements can be seriously distorted by changes in accounting methods. In this connection it should be observed that there is an increasing and laudable tendency on the part of corporations who have changed accounting procedures to rework at least the significant figures for the preceding five or ten years and to publish the data on both the old and the new basis.

Of perhaps greater significance is the fact that the extremely different values which result from the use of different accounting methods make it virtually impossible to evaluate claims (and counterclaims) that corporation profits are too low (or too high) relative to demands for increased wages, increased dividends, lower prices, or whatever happens to be the issue of the moment. Beyond this, of course, is the obvious possibility for the judicious and unannounced selection of a different accounting method to suggest that operating results were better (or worse) than would be indicated by different accounting methods. In general, this possibility has been severely restricted by the fact that the public accountant's certificate states that statements are prepared on a "consistent basis," and the practice of accountants to take exception in their certificate when this is not the case.

Thus, there is some protection against deliberate abuse of the uncertain state of accounting procedure. There is no protection against the destruction of comparability which results from this lack of uniformity. There are two fairly obvious remedies for this situation: some sort of enforced uniformity of procedure, or a complete disclosure of accounting methods used as an integral part of any accounting statement.

Since the second of these remedies seems vastly less efficacious, it will be briefly discussed now before turning major attention to the much more important possibility of enforced uniformity. The objective of full disclosure of accounting methods used would presumably be to enable the user of the report to make it comparable with other reports by adjusting various results for different methods used. If disclosure of method is not to provide for the possibility of comparability there would seem to be no particular reason for the disclosure.

The most obvious difficulty with this procedure is that unless it is assumed that all users of accounting reports were quite familiar with accounting procedure and terminology, useful disclosure would probably require something approaching an accounting manual. The very detail required to make the disclosure of method useful to users of the statements would be so involved that it would be virtually useless.

Secondly, it is doubtful that disclosure of *method* alone would be sufficient to make possible the adjustments necessary for comparability. In a great many instances these adjustments could only be made with information about *method* and about *amounts* involved. A trained accountant or analyst would know in a general way the result of using any one of the several depreciation methods, for example; but without data on cost, age, and expected life of the plant (and all other plant and equipment) he could not convert the results to those which would be obtained with another method. In other words, to make comparability effective, reports would have to include not only disclosure of procedures used but, in addition, the results which would be obtained from different procedures. All in all, disclosure of accounting methods used does not seem a very useful way of overcoming the problem created by lack of uniformity.

The arguments against enforced uniformity have been stated on many occasions. The nearest thing to an official argument is found in the introduction to the accounting research bulletins of the American Institute of Certified Public Accountants:

> Uniformity has usually connoted similar treatment of the same item occurring in many cases, in which sense it runs the risk of concealing important differences among cases. Another sense of the word would require that different authorities working independently on the same case should reach the same conclusions. Although uniformity is a worthwhile goal, it should not be pursued to the exclusion of other benefits. Changes of emphasis and objective as well as changes in conditions under which business operates have led, and doubtless will continue to lead, to the adoption of new accounting procedures. Consequently diversity of practice may continue as new practices are adopted before old ones are completely discarded.[4]

Mr. Marquis Eaton, in the address quoted from before, suggested:

> It would be a great misfortune for American business, and the whole economy, if uniform accounting rules were to be prescribed by governmental fiat. It would probably mean the end of progress. The Interstate Commerce Commission did exactly this in 1914 for the regulated railroads. At the time the I.C.C. accounting classification was hailed as reflecting the best accounting thought of the day. It was cited as a model in accounting textbooks. By 1957 it was completely out of date—far behind the financial reporting standards of industrial corporations.

The essential arguments against uniformity thus seem to be the fear that it would conceal important differences and, most important, that it would stifle the development of accounting.

As far as concealing differences is concerned, this would only happen with a degree of uniformity which no one of whom the

---

[4]American Institute of Certified Public Accountants, *Accounting Research and Terminology Bulletins* (final ed., New York, 1961), pp. 7-8.

writer is aware has ever contemplated. For example, uniformity does not imply that industries such as tobacco and distilled liquor which have very special inventory problems would have to account for these in exactly the same way as industries which do not have these problems. The automobile manufacturers have to contend with immense tooling costs; steel makers have to account for the periodic rebuilding of furnaces; oil companies have underground reserves. Uniformity would simply mean these particular cases would be accounted for in a uniform fashion by those who have the particular problem. It would in no way involve other corporations in these problems. On the other hand, uniformity would presumably mean, for example, that all ordinary industrial plant and equipment would be accounted for in the same fashion. There seems no reason to believe that this would conceal *truly* important differences.

Mr. Eaton is not the only commentator to have cited the *Uniform System of Accounts for Class I Railroads* of the Interstate Commerce Commission as an illustration of the evils of enforced uniformity in accounting. I have, in the past, been a severe critic of this particular system,[5] but its particular weaknesses are not necessarily relevant to the broader situation being discussed here. The reasons for stagnation in the railroad industry are many and varied. Undoubtedly the accounting system has been one among these, but just as surely some of the other factors have been reasons for stagnation in the thinking of railroad accountants both in the companies and in the ICC.

Furthermore, it is important to recognize that the ICC system is, in the first instance, a system of *bookkeeping* rather than a system of *accounting*. That system sets forth in extreme detail rules for recording literally thousands of transactions. There is no doubt that this sort of uniformity would stifle even the most vivid imagination, but such a system is a far cry from enforcing a degree of uniformity in reporting on such things as inventory, depreciation, and intangibles. Experience with the railroad ac-

---

[5]In *Cost Data for the Management of Railroad Passenger Service* (Boston: Division of Research, Harvard Business School, 1957), chap. IV.

counting system is not really relevant to the question of uniformity in reporting.

The Committee on Accounting Research suggests that changes in conditions have led and will continue to lead to changes in accounting methods. There seems no good reason to believe that those who might have responsibility for enforcing uniformity would be any less aware of these changes than would those actually doing the reporting. Furthermore, in addition to the thousands of practicing accountants there are hundreds of accounting professors in the nation's colleges and universities. If even a tiny portion of these latter are doing their jobs as they should there will be no failure of recognition of changed conditions, no lack of suggestions for new and better methods.

The present system has been described as follows:

New developments in accounting principles and related practices, in general, go through transitional periods as a result of an evolutionary process. This process tends to follow a course that might be divided into five transitional phases. . . .

These transitional phases have occurred and are occurring, usually over a period of many years. . . . While it is recognized that an evolutionary type of transition usually cannot be accomplished quickly and that a period of experimentation may be necessary, some of the transitional hurdles are simply road blocks that favor the status quo. The public accountant's responsibility for meeting today's accelerated pace of business development may not permit leisurely transition periods of ten to fifteen years or longer.[6]

The present system of development of accounting procedures is rather like the New England attic—nothing is ever thrown out. Surely this results in part from inertia—from an unwillingness to change procedures which have worked in the past—a characteristic no more prevalent among accountants than among any other group. It also results, no doubt, from an unwillingness to undertake an often difficult explanation of apparent changes in operating results or in values which result from changes in accounting procedures. Above all, it results

---

[6]Arthur Anderson & Co., *Accounting and Reporting Problems of the Accounting Profession* (Chicago, 1960), pp. 3-4.

from a lack of discipline among that very widespread group who develops accounting ideas and puts them to use, a matter discussed more fully in Chapter Twelve.

One reason for reluctance to change accounting methods which is rarely articulated but is nevertheless a strong deterrent is the relatively large change in amounts which changes in method may involve. For example, the Imperial Tobacco Company of Canada, the largest tobacco manufacturer in Canada, restated its land, buildings, and equipment from historical cost to replacement cost in 1961. This restatement involved an increase of over $25 million—from $58 million to $83 million. Obviously such a change in amounts from one year to the next has a tremendous impact. Even with a great deal of careful explanation of objectives, methods, and adjustments (and Imperial Tobacco gave a generally excellent explanation) the likelihood of uncertainty in a reader's mind cannot be denied.

On the other hand, it must be remembered that these large changes will occur only once. Subsequent changes will reflect only the normal change in values as stated on the new basis. In the case of Imperial Tobacco, the increase in replacement value of land, plant, and equipment between 1960 and 1961 was only about $600,000, part of which was accounted for by net increase in resources held. In the case of price-level adjustments (to be discussed below), it would require an essential doubling of the monetary amount of an asset held since 1945 to account for the roughly 50 per cent decline in the purchasing power of money since that time. After this initial adjustment was made, however, subsequent adjustments would need only account for the current annual rate of decline in purchasing power, say 2 per cent to 3 per cent.

The initial adjustment of monetary sums often required by a change in accounting methods is a matter which requires a careful and full explanation by those who prepare the statements. Readers of statements must, in turn, accept the obligation to make the effort to understand the changes and particularly to understand that the magnitude of the difference is not indicative of a similar change in the immediate, short-run status of the corporation. That these requirements for explanation and under-standing can be met must be assumed and the magnitude of the initial difference resulting from changes in accounting method not allowed to prevent needed improvements.

Changing Price Levels

The fact of changing price levels is too well known to require elaboration. During the years since World War II, the pur-chasing power of the dollar has declined by about 50 per cent, and since the dollar is the basis of virtually all accounting mea-surements the implications are obvious. For example, assume that a company acquired an asset in year x for $100,000. A second company acquiring an exact duplicate of the asset one year later, because of a decline in the purchasing power of money, would have paid $120,000 for it. These sums are included among the accounting listings of each company's assets, and all else being equal a reader of the statements would conclude that the second company was worth more than the first. By any reasonable definition of "worth" this is manifestly not so.

The other side of this coin is seen in any consideration of the sources of the funds used to acquire the company's assets. Gen-erally speaking, in our past two decades of inflation the debtor has been in a favorable postion because his obligation to repay is based on the value of money at the time he incurred the debt. As the value of money decreases these fixed payments become less and less of a burden to the debtor. Thus, the postion of a company with a debt of $100,000 acquired in 1950 may be quite different from the position of a company with the same amount of debt taken on in 1955.

The effects of inflation upon profit determination are dis-cussed in some detail in a subsequent chapter. For the moment, it is sufficient to point out that for the most part a company's revenues will be in current dollars while expenses currently being deducted from these revenues may well represent past expenditures of quite different dollars. Thus, the operating re-sults of the two otherwise identical companies may be quite different depending on when the dollars currently being charged off were actually spent.

The continued ignoring of changing dollar *values* means that the dollar *amounts* of a company's assets may be quite meaningless in terms of current dollar values and in terms of comparisons with other companies. The same is true of a company's debt. The conventional calculation of profit may result in quite distorted figures when no recognition is given to changing dollar values.

This situation has probably received more discussion than any other aspect of accounting in the past fifteen or so years. At the same time perhaps less has been done about it than about any of the other problems of accounting. The big surge of inflation in 1947 and 1948 led to a vast amount of discussion and some limited action. Some corporations such as Chrysler and U. S. Steel made adjustments of depreciation charges (which, of course, only get at one aspect of the problem) in their annual reports. The American Institute of Certified Public Accountants[7] through its Committee on Accounting Procedures, disapproved of these limited attempts to deal with the situation and, by implication, with other, more vigorous action.

> While there are differences of opinion, the prevailing sentiment in these groups [businessmen, bankers, economists, labor leaders and others] is against any basic change in accounting procedures. The committee believes that such a change would confuse readers of financial statements and nullify many of the gains that have been made toward clearer presentation of corporate finances.[8]

In 1951 the American Accounting Association's Committee on Concepts and Standards issued a statement encouraging the use of supplementary statements in which monetary amounts were adjusted for changes in monetary values. This group felt that experimentation was needed before the best way of dealing with the situation could be determined.[9]

---

[7]American Institute of Certified Public Accountants, *Accounting Research and Terminology Bulletin* (final ed., New York, 1961), chap. 9.

[8]*Ibid.*, p. 69.

[9]American Accounting Association, *Price Level Changes and Financial Statements, Supplementary Statement No. 2* (1951).

More or less as a result of this call for experimentation, the association with grants from the Merrill Foundation sponsored a study of four companies, directed by Professor Ralph C. Jones of Yale. This study, published in 1955, indicated that the distortion in accounting values, created by a failure to adjust for changing monetary values, was substantial indeed.[10] While this study left little room for doubt that inflation (and the deflation of the 1930's, too) made accounting statements with unadjusted dollar amounts virtually meaningless, it did not generate any significant change in accounting practice generally. Indeed, in June, 1959, Mr. Carmen Blough, then director of research of the AICPA, stated:

> However, though I acknowledge the soundness of complete adjustment for price-level changes as a matter of principle or theory I do not feel that it is practical at this time. How far must inflation go before it would be practical? I do not know but it would have to be far enough for its significance to be understood by many more than understand it today.[11]

In 1961, Professor Moonitz, successor to Mr. Blough as research director of the AICPA, was urging that the 1951 proposals of the American Accounting Association for experimentation with supplementary statements adjusted for price-level changes be implemented.[12] As those of the gods, the mills of accounting grind slowly.

The stated arguments against the adjustment of accounting data seem to center on three points: (1) there has not yet been enough inflation to make the problem critical; (2) neither a general index, such as a Consumer Price Index, nor a special index is very exact; (3) statements given in adjusted dollars are difficult to understand. Among the unstated arguments the inertia and reluctance to change referred to above no doubt loom large.

---

[10]Ralph C. Jones, *Price Level Changes and Financial Statements, Case Studies of Four Companies* (American Accounting Association, 1955).

[11]From an address before the National Association of Accountants, New York, June, 1959.

[12]Maurice Moonitz, *The Basic Postulates of Accounting* (New York: American Institute of Certified Public Accountants, 1961), pp. 44-46.

The first of these arguments is entirely subjective, of course. The evidence of the Jones study and a more recent study by E. S. Hendricksen[13] indicate there has been enough inflation to distort seriously accounting results. When adjusted statements, as in the case of Armstrong Cork Company, show that average return on equity was 4.5 per cent compared with 8.8 per cent shown by unadjusted statements,[14] one might reasonably conclude there has been more than enough inflation to warrant taking positive action.

The statement that the Consumer Price Index or some other index is not exact is, of course, quite true. It is also a completely irrelevant argument because it is based on the assumption that what the index would replace is itself exact. This assumption is quite false for it is certain that unadjusted dollar amounts in a period of fluctuating monetary values are wrong. The use of an index to adjust dollar values, then, can be said to substitute some probability of being approximately correct for the virtual certainty of being absolutely wrong.

In this connection, it is of interest to note that several European governments publish official indexes for use by companies in adjusting monetary values in connection with the calculation of taxable income. (These indexes are developed specifically for various classes of machinery and equipment. Some writers have argued that such indexes only partly measure monetary inflation and are partly measuring improvements or changes in the particular equipment, that is, measuring replacement value. A general index, such as the Consumer Price Index, is often recommended on the grounds that it gives the best measure of general inflation as such.)

The fact that adjusted data are more difficult to understand is undeniable, but this is not a good reason for failing to correct a manifestly bad situation. After all, many people still do not understand the parable of the talents but this did not prevent Jesus from telling it to us. In general, it must be assumed that

---

[13]E. S. Hendricksen, *Price-Level Adjustments of Financial Statements* (Pullman, Wash.: Washington State University Press, 1961).

[14]Ralph C. Jones, *op. cit.*, p. 67.

most people involved in evaluating corporations' performances are reasonably intelligent and reasonably well educated. Investment dealers, union officials, Representatives and Senators, journalists, university professors, government officials will either be well able to contemplate data adjusted for price-level changes or will have ready access to staff members who are. And once again in this connection, one must ask whether it is not better to educate people to manage difficult concepts than to mislead them with the false assurance of simple concepts.

Summary

Contemporary accounting practice offers the accountant a fairly wide and essentially free choice of rules and procedures for dealing with most accounting problems. Accounting bases most of its measurement on the monetary unit, and in general practicing accountants have not taken steps to eliminate the effects of inflation on the monetary unit. Thus, there is relatively little comparability among the periodic reports of single enterprises, nor is it possible to make reasonable comparisons among the reports of several corporations.

It must be recognized that neither last year's performance of Company A nor this year's performance of Company B are necessarily valid criteria for evaluating this year's performance of Company A. On the other hand, such comparisons are an important part of the evaluatory process. The usefulness of the information typically available about corporations is seriously limited by the variety of accounting procedures and by the failure to eliminate effects of price-level changes.

Chapter Five

THE PROCEDURAL BASES
OF ACCOUNTING

I

Accounting for the large modern corporation involves the accountant in a dual role. One role, which has dominated the preceding discussions, is as a means of communication between corporation managements and properly interested outsiders. In its second role accounting is a system of measurement, measuring the results of the myriad of financial transactions which are in turn the reflection of a wide range of business decisions and actions. That accounting's role is dual should not be lost sight of, for it is simultaneously measurer and communicator. What it communicates is largely determined by how it measures, and how it measures must be determined by what it intends to communicate.

II

In terms of both measurement and communication it is essential to recognize that there are necessary and desirable limits upon the phenomena with which accounting can deal. Accountants have generally maintained that they are concerned only with *financial* matters, with those phenomena susceptible to measurement in financial terms. Thus accounting would not attempt to measure and report upon such things as employee satisfaction, the wisdom of a pricing policy, the taste of advertising, etc. Behavioral scientists with long training and experience have difficulty measuring employee satisfaction. Economists debate pricing policy at length. Advertising is quarreled over and "researched" constantly by experts and laymen with little more than confirmation of one's prejudices as a result. All these matters are sufficiently remote from the background and training of most accountants to make these self-imposed prohibitions perfectly sound and appropriate.

It is appropriate that accounting has limited itself to financial matters, but it is unfortunate that the limits around what shall be considered as financial matters have, in practice, been very narrowly defined. Cash on hand is clearly a financial resource and so are inventories of materials or goods for sale. There is no question that plant and equipment are resources. But what of a trade-mark such as "Coca-Cola" or "Ivory Soap"? And what of the partly formed idea for an ultimately successful product in the mind of a chemist or engineer in the research laboratory? Or what of the imagination, intelligence, and skill of the president who directs the company? Most would agree that all these are very significant resources. Indeed, in this day when many companies can *make* a great variety of things with equal speed and efficiency, it seems that those factors which lead to the development of new things to make and to the speedy and efficient distribution of these things are at least equal in importance to raw materials and production machinery. Accounting, however, has continued to give most of its attention to the resources used in making things—usually referred to as tangible assets—and, of course, to monetary assets such as cash, accounts receivable, and securities. Accountants have not said that these other, intangible assets are nonfinancial and therefore beyond the limits of accounting, but by failing to give much serious attention to the difficult problem of valuing them the result is much the same: many intangible resources are not valued and not recognized. Some specific problems of accounting for intangibles are discussed in Chapter Eleven. For the moment it is enough to recognize that in practice accounting has unfortunately limited itself to so-called tangible assets, even though we recognize the widsom of the broader limitation to financial matters.

It is also important to recognize the essentially subjective nature of the conventions and rules underlying the theory and practice of accounting. Most measurement systems with which we are familiar are based on natural laws or physical relationships derived from the phenomena being measured. There are no such laws or relationships in business transactions, nor are the phenomena themselves necessarily manifest. Capital and income, for example, are matters of definition and thus are debatable and debated. Accountants are therefore forced simultaneously to define the phenomena they are measuring and to establish rules or accepted procedures or conventions for making the measurements. (Traditionally these have been called the principles and postulates of accounting and there has been quite a bit of semantic argument about whether the measurements are based on postulates or principles. A different term "convention" will be used here because it seems most appropriate. The Merriam-Webster defines conventions as rules and practices which have as their sanction custom and usage and it is on exactly such that accounting is based.)

These conventions are essentially the practical and considered responses of the persons who first used and articulated them to the nature of the job they had to do and to the circumstances surrounding the job including, no doubt, their own attitudes. For example, consider the convention of conservatism which is generally taken to mean that when there is uncertainty and choice, resources should be undervalued rather than overvalued, income should be understated rather than overstated. Surely such a convention reflects a state of mind rather than a necessarily natural or obvious basis for measurement. That conservatism has general acceptance as a factor in measurement reflects the fact that the men who proposed it in the first place were conservative men, and its continued acceptance is surely because the men who have followed them in accounting are conservative men. Were the radicals in the population attracted to accounting, the convention would surely be different.

There has been some evolution and much discussion of these conventions over the years, but basically they have remained unchanged for some time in spite of great changes in the nature of the accountant's job. This continued acceptance of these conventions should reflect the considered opinions of those who have continued to accept and use them that they are still valid responses to the nature of the job to be done and to the circumstances which surround it. Perhaps it does. One may, however, at least suggest the possibility that the basically subjective origin of these conventions has been lost sight of and that they have become dogma not because of any inherent validity but simply because of general and continued usage. In the following pages, those accounting conventions which seem to have continuing validity are briefly described.

III

Consistency

Consistency in accounting means that accounting policies and procedures should be the same over a succession of accounting periods. To the extent that the idea of consistency prevents the making of capricious and short-run changes in accounting and reporting, it may be useful. Beyond this, however, it frequently serves as a cloak behind which those who are reluctant to change can hide. Progress in accounting and consistency in accounting are not always compatible.

Materiality

The convention of materiality simply means that all material or significant transactions, values, and contingencies should be disclosed in accounting reports. The converse, of course, is that such reports should not be cluttered with immaterial or insignificant data. How influential this convention has been to date is indicated by the fact that millions of dollars of intangible but important resources go unaccounted for in financial reports that carry the "value" of unexpired fire-insurance premiums to the exact penny. Because of the importance of accounting's role in communicating business facts to outsiders avoidance of the sin of omission is most necessary. Because communication cannot be very effective unless it is understandable, the sin of commission is as much to be avoided.

Money

The role of money in accounting is, as the role of money elsewhere is generally thought to be, a matter of considerable virtue and a source of considerable evil. The virtue of money is that it provides accountants with an absolutely essential lowest common denominator. It is only through description in equivalent monetary terms that the "shoes and ships and sealing wax/cabbages and [presidents]" or any other of an infinite number of combinations of things which are the stuff of a modern corporation can be compared and analyzed. Since costs are hours of labor, barrels of nails, martinis at lunch, and a tremendous variety of other elements, income can be contemplated only after all the diverse elements of revenue and cost have been reduced to common monetary terms. Without the ability to express a great range of business facts on a common monetary basis, accounting would not be possible.

The evils brought on by the use of money are two. In the first place money is generally quite unstable. Much of the confusion which surrounds the appraisal of corporate performance is occasioned by the instability of money over time. We have lived for a very long time with generally rising price levels and it is not certain that this will significantly change in the future. Thus it must be recognized that the use of monetary equivalents in accounting is grossly misleading unless specific provision is made for its instability. (See preceding chapter.)

Money values, because they are numbers, can be readily manipulated with a high degree of elegance and precision, a fact which does not change but often obscures the essential subjectivity of much of accounting. Depending on the definition of cost used, a particular resource may be given values the greatest of which might be 100 per cent or more of the lowest. Carrying such values to the nearest penny simply because it is arithmetically possible does nothing more than create a most unsound illusion of objectivity. In our era of great change, and as a result of the vastly increased scope of corporate responsibilties, the monetary concept must not be permitted to obscure, as it often does, the uncertainty and subjectivity surrounding much of accounting.

Money is a convenient way of expressing financial facts and the use of money as the basic device is most appropriate. However, it must be recognized that failure to adjust changes in the value of money makes the monetary convention utterly misleading. It further needs to be recognized that in spite of the fact that money values can be added and subtracted, multiplied and divided, they represent in a great many cases essentially subjective and uncertain conclusions.

Permanence

Strictly speaking, the life of a corporation is, at any particular point in time, of uncertain duration. Corporate charters are granted for periods of, for example, 99 years, 999 years, or simply indefinite periods, but the hopes and expectations of founders do not influence the sometimes harsh realities of the market place. Thus, a corporation may cease to exist at once or shortly thereafter or it may continue on indefinitely, and accounting for its current status under either of these conditions will be significantly different. (Resources which have great value when used by an operating business in the production of goods and services often have little or no value when put on the market directly because they cannot be used for other purposes.) Consequently, it has been necessary to make some convenient assumption about this matter of the life of the corporation being accounted for. From this need has come the going-concern or permanence convention which simply states the assumption that a corporation will continue to operate for an indefinitely long period in the future. The assumption would not be made in the face of specific knowledge of imminent liquidation, of course. In terms of the corporations which are the concern of this book, such an assumption is completely reasonable. The average life span of all American corporations is fairly short, but the odds

43

that General Electric, Traveler's Insurance, U. S. Steel and the like will continue to exist indefinitely are overwhelming.

Unfortunately, this convention of permanence can be interpreted in the two essentially opposite ways illustrated in the following statement.

The importance of the permanence assumption can be indicated by contrasting it with a possible alternative; namely, that the business is about to be liquidated or sold. Under the latter assumption accounting would attempt to measure at all times what the business is currently worth to a buyer, but under the going-concern assumption there is no need to do this, and it is in fact not done.[1]

There is a subtle but nonetheless important distinction between the *liquidation* of a business and the *sale* of a business. Treating these together is a result of accounting's traditional exclusive emphasis on the ownership interest for from the point of view of the owner there is no significant difference between them, assuming the amount of cash he receives is the same. However, from the point of view of all the other groups who have an interest in the corporation there are significant differences. For management and workers it is the striking difference between continued employment and being out of work. For customers it is the difference between being able to continue with a source of supply and having to look for a new one. For the public in general it may be a question of the continuation or not of an important economic institution. Accounting which is to serve interests other than those of the stockholder must distinguish between the liquidation of a business and the sale of a going-concern.

It has already been implied that both the responsibilities and objectives of the modern large corporation are such that appraisal of their status and progress must be based on current values. This point will be made explicit in Chapter Six. The acceptance of the convention of permanence to preclude accounting in terms of liquidation is appropriate and useful. It

---

[1]R. N. Anthony, *Management Accounting* (rev. ed.; Homewood, Ill.: Richard D. Irwin, Inc., 1960), p. 30.

should not be used to support unwarranted and misleading emphasis on the past, an emphasis which destroys much of the usefulness of accounting as a basis for such appraisals.

Income Taxation

Even though it is only marginally related to the matter of accounting conventions, this seems a useful place to discuss in general terms the relationship between accounting and income taxation. There is no doubt that the taxation of income has had a great deal of influence upon accounting, especially since the mid-1930's when the rates of taxation first became of significant size. Given that a tax is to be levied on income, accounting for that income becomes critical for the very obvious reason that the amount of tax to be paid is a direct function of the amount of income. The use of an accounting procedure which will lower net income means, quite literally, money in the bank. There is no doubt that the adoption of the income tax greatly increased the opportunities of employment for accountants and gave powerful stimulus to the accountant's emphasis on income determination.

In the beginning it was generally intended that the income tax would be based on corporate income as conventionally defined. However, there are a number of considerations involved in the levying of a tax which have no relevance to any accepted definitions of corporate income, and consequently the definition of taxable income has, over the years, moved farther and farther away from corporate income.

Income taxation is increasingly used as a tool in implementing the economic and social policies of the government. For example, the taxable income of an oil-producing company which includes an essentially political deduction for depletion would satisfy no accounting definition of income. Income-tax regulations must also be concerned with equity, which is not of concern in accounting. The exclusion of dividends received by a corporation from that corporation's taxable income may represent equitable treatment of that corporation's stockholders, but it is at odds with any accepted basis for income determination. Nor are these

45

broad social functions of tax policy likely to change. In 1962, the estimated useful lives of fixed assets generally accepted by the Treasury Department as the basis for computing depreciation deductions for tax purposes were generally shortened. This is an avowed device to stimulate new investment in plant and equipment and thereby to stimulate the nation's economy. This does not mean that the basis for computing depreciation for corporate accounting purposes should be changed in the same way. The government is really not concerned with taxing income as such. It is interested in collecting needed revenues without doing unnecessary damage to the economy and it can and does manipulate the basis for taxation with this objective in view, quite without concern over whether the resulting base is, in fact, income as usually defined.

Many changes are needed to make accounting more nearly appropriate to its role as the source of data upon which to base appraisals of the way the modern corporation is meeting its manifold responsibilities. These changes will inevitably magnify the differences between taxable income and corporate income beyond what they are at present. Consequently, it is not only desirable but necessary to recognize that income tax concerns income in name only and to end its influence on accounting concepts and procedures.

Past and Future

It is less convention than necessity which forces accounting to be primarily historical. The line between reporting facts and fortune telling is not always easy to draw, yet it must be recognized. On the other hand, one must also recognize the relative relevance of the past and the future in the process of appraising corporate performance. Basically, data relating to the past can serve as a basis for rewards and punishments. They can also, on occasion, serve as rough guides to the future. However, the nature of many corporations is changing so rapidly in response to changes in technology and in the generally held view of their role and responsibility that past data quickly lose their significance.

A real evaluation of corporate status and progress can be made only on the basis of the *expected* results of contemplated *future* actions. By and large, businessmen make their own decisions on the basis of such information, and the *current* capital commitments, *future* income, and *future* funds flow are key pieces of information in these decisions. Ideally, those concerned with appraising the effectiveness of such decisions should have the same information.

There are obvious implications—competitive and otherwise—in including income budgets and funds-flow projections in corporation reports. In the first place, a considerable amount of uncertainty is generally inherent in such budgets or projections and it is probably unrealistic to expect that many who would use these data could or perhaps would make adequate provision for this uncertainty. The fact that actual performance varies from projected performance may result from poor management, but it may also be an indication of a poor, or simply unfortunate, forecast. Interpretation of results requires a degree of sophistication and discretion which might not always be available. Furthermore, the "giving away of plans" which would be involved in making such forecasts and projections available would certainly have the effect of limiting whatever competition is left in our system, although if the practice were universally followed no particular corporation would be put at a disadvantage.

For these reasons alone, to suggest that budgets or forecasts of income and funds flow be included in corporation reports is certainly premature and probably impractical. On the other hand, it needs to be recognized that real control over the use of resources can only come before the resources are committed, and the decision to commit them to a particular use must be based on an evaluation of *expected* results. Certainly the steady growth of corporate influence and responsibilities demands that accountants begin to develop procedures by which income budgets and funds-flow projections can be communicated to those to whom the corporations are responsible—procedures which will make allowance for uncertainty and provide for the protection of desired competition.

One may accept the present practical barriers to communication to outsiders of estimates of future progress without obviating the need of those outsiders for information oriented toward the future. A readily available step in the direction of meeting this need is to make sure that the conventional summary statements—balance sheet, income statement, funds-flow statement—focus on the present rather than on the largely irrelevant past. One step towards this objective is the adjustment of monetary values discussed in another connection in Chapter Four. This would, of course, have the effect of eliminating monetary values left over from an irrelevant and irredeemable past from accounting statements. They would then at least be related to the present, which is the beginning of the future. Another principal step involves reconsidering some of the basic definitions underlying the determination of value and the measurement of income. This matter is discussed in Chapter Six. Here again, the objective should be to have the accounting statements as current as possible. As will be suggested, this will require some fairly major changes in currently popular conventions and procedures, but if one accepts that there have already been major changes in the broad social and economic role of the organizations being accounted for, the requirement for change in accounting is not something to choke upon.

IV

Accounting is limited to informing interested outsiders about only a part of the total spectrum of business affairs. Also, some uncertainty is inherent in accounting's bases for measurement. Useful accounting must be concerned with the future, yet accounting must avoid idle speculation and limit itself to reasonably supportable statements. Unfortunately, the precise extent of these limitations and uncertainties is not clear, and thus there is always room for disagreement and continued discussion. It seems safe to say that no one will ever produce a definitive solution to the twin problems of what and how accounting should measure and communicate. On the other hand, it seems clear that the only worthwhile approach to these problems starts from accounting's role as a link between the corporation and those to whom it is responsible. Conventions, procedures, and rules for communication and measurement will make sense only if they are derived from the needs of those at each end of the chain of responsibility. Broadly speaking, these needs, as suggested earlier, are met by putting into the hands of interested outsiders—stockholders, employees, customers, suppliers, and the public—information which will help them to make a significant evaluation of the current status and probable future progress of the corporation and, in turn, help to establish the legitimacy of management.

Chapter Six

VALUE AND CAPITAL

I

The single most important task of accounting is determining the value of the various resources or of the capital of the corporation. (These two terms—resources and capital—are at one point completely synonymous. A corporation's capital is the aggregate of all its resources. The aggregate of the resources of the corporation is its capital.) These values are the foundation of all that accounting does. Capital, both in terms of individual resources and in the aggregate, is the essence of the balance sheet. Similarly, it is the essence of the funds statement because that description of changes in the sources and uses of capital must obviously start with valuation of the capital. Income arises as a result of the conversion of resources into goods and services and the distribution of goods and services. The amount of net income depends upon the values given to the resources disposed of and to the resources received in exchange. While problems of accounting measurement are often discussed in other terms, in virtually all cases they revolve around the question of value. In this chapter, several different definitions of value or of capital which have some currency in accounting practice or literature are considered.

II

The only true measure of the value of a resource is the goods or services or other satisfactions which will result from its possession or use in the future. In terms of the resources held by a corporation, their value is their present worth, which may be defined as the present value of the net receipts to be received in the future from the use of the resources, discounted at a rate appropriate to the risk involved in this use. Thus, by definition, the capital of a corporation would be equal to the aggregate of the present worth of all its resources. Periodic income would be measured by comparing the amount of capital held at the beginning of the period with the amount of capital held at the end of the period. The change in present worth (after allowing for new investment from outside the corporation and for distribution of value to investors) would be net income (or loss). It is also important that net income thus defined would, before any distributions, be exactly equal to growth achieved through operations or through holding resources.

In terms of an appraisal of corporate status, present worth is a most appropriate basis for valuation. If the function of a corporation is to utilize most effectively the resources it controls, present worth has the merit of being the only basis for comparing all of the opportunities for using the resources. Present worth is completely forward looking, and the future is the only really relevant consideration in terms of control over the use of resources. An increase in present worth is, as suggested above, a precise measure of growth, a matter of considerable significance if the objective of corporation managers is to achieve growth. In terms of the responsibilities and apparent objectives of the large modern corporation, present worth provides a most suitable definition of value and capital.

Unfortunately, however, a great deal of uncertainty is involved in the projection of future net receipts. It must also be recognized that there is a great deal of subjectivity involved in establishing the amount of risk related to a particular course of action. The uncertainty and the subjectivity can be, and frequently are, managed in valuations made by businessmen making investment decisions within the firm. This is possible because the men involved are few in number and in general are, or should be, intimately familiar with the risks and uncertainties involved in their particular firm. The theory of probability is well developed and its applications in the type of situation being discussed here are becoming more and more understood. However, the conceptual and operational difficulties involved are so great that at the present time it is premature to recommend the present-value basis for accounting for corporate resources in reports and statements for interested outsiders. Present worth of future receipts can be accepted as the theoretically correct and desirable approach to resource valuation and at the same time rejected on the practical grounds that at the present time it is virtually impossible to implement in a satisfactory manner.

III

Because practical implementation of the theoretically correct definition of capital and value as the present worth of resources held is not possible, one must look to other definitions. The three definitions of capital and value, each of which has some role either explicit or implicit in contemporary accounting, are *monetary*, *purchasing power*, and *productive capacity*.

Monetary

The most generally used and commonly understood definition of value and capital is *monetary*. That is, the capital of a corporation is a stock of money or monetary equivalents of other resources which has flowed into the corporation from creditors, stockholders, profitable operations, or other sources. The value of any of a corporation's resources would be equal to the amount of money given in exchange for them. This is the "value-equals-original-monetary-cost" convention which is deeply imbedded in current accounting practice. Net income would be realized only after the stock of monetary capital had been restored out of the revenue of the period. Put another way, net income would be equal to the difference between revenue earned and the original monetary cost of goods and services consumed in producing the gross revenue.

For the most part, implementation of the monetary definition of capital and value is extremely simple. One works primarily with the record of money or money obligations given or received. In the case of income determination one must deal with the problem created by the use of assets over relatively long periods of time. In these cases it becomes necessary to determine how much of the total value of the asset is a cost of a particular period. However, since total value equals total cost in this case the problem is somewhat simplified and, as suggested in Chapter Three, current accounting practice, which focuses its attention almost exclusively on income determination, results in balance-sheet values which are simply the residuals of original cost not charged against income. (This question is discussed at some length in Chapters Seven and Eight.)

Purchasing Power

The successive waves of inflation in the years after 1945 directed much attention to what may be called the *purchasing-power* definition of capital. In this case the capital of a corporation is viewed as being a stock of purchasing power, expressed in monetary terms, received from all sources. Thus, the value of any resource would equal the *current* purchasing power given in exchange for it. Net income would not be realized until the stock of purchasing power consumed in producing the gross income had been restored out of gross income. Net income would be equal to the difference between revenue earned in current purchasing power and incurred cost, which is defined as the monetary equivalent of the purchasing power consumed in producing the gross income. The determination of cost again involves the problem of long-lived assets, and in this case the cost for a particular period would simply be based on the current purchasing power equivalent of the original cost of the asset in question.

The purchasing-power view of capital requires a regular revision of the value of resources held—at least to the extent that the purchasing power of money changes. At the time capital is received or committed to a particular use, money and purchasing power are equal. However, if money changes in value subsequently, the amount of purchasing power represented by the capital, stated in monetary terms, will change. With 10 per cent inflation, for example, a particular resource which initially represented the giving up of $100,000 in purchasing power will now come to have represented $110,000 in purchasing power and the resource would be revalued accordingly.

Changes in purchasing power may be measured by one of a number of general price-level indexes or by indexes specifically based upon the corporation's own resources. The general arguments for and against the use of price-level indexes in accounting were presented in Chapter Four. Their use is not without difficulty both in terms of operation and of understanding, but it is essential to an implementation of the purchasing-power definition of capital.

Productive Capacity

A corporation's capital may also be defined as a stock of *productive capacity*. Productive capacity is not used here in the narrow sense of making things but in the broader sense of acquiring, manufacturing, and distributing goods or services. Such a view postulates that the capital of a corporation is a stock of resources—money, inventories, facilities, manpower, etc.—which came into the corporation from the usual sources—creditors, stockholders, profitable operations, etc. In this view, the value of any particular resource or the value of all resources is represented by the amount of money currently required to replace them. There would be no net income until the stock of productive capacity consumed had been restored out of the gross income. Put another way, the costs of producing the revenue earned would be the cost of replacing the goods and services consumed. Costs arising from the use of long-lived assets would in this instance be based on the current replacement value of the asset used.

Implementation of this definition of capital requires the restatement of monetary equivalents whenever the replacement cost of a resource changes. Replacement cost cannot be measured with the simple precision characteristic of the measurement of historical monetary values. In the latter case a receipted bill establishes value once and for all. For those resources regularly bought and sold in an established market, replacement value is as easy to establish as is current market price. For resources such as land and buildings, replacement value can be estimated quite readily by qualified appraisers. In some instances, indexes of labor and material and other costs may be the basis for an estimate of replacement value.

IV

The competitive-capacity view of capital and its twin, the replacement-cost view of value are, of the three different definitions of capital and value, the most appropriate for current use on both theoretical and practical grounds. On theoretical grounds replacement cost has validity because in general the current price at which any particular resource is being bought and sold should give a fair approximation of its present worth to either buyer or seller. (This generalization must be somewhat modified by the existence of differing utilities. A lathe may have greater value for a machine shop which is rejecting orders because of lack of capacity than for a machine shop which is under capacity.) In those instances where replacement value must be estimated, the basis on which the estimations are made must contemplate the existence of buyers and sellers, which inevitably involves approaching present value. There are, of course, some instances where the resource in question is quite irreplaceable—such things as brand names, exclusive distribution systems, and the like, for example. In these cases, the idea of productive capacity, as defined, is not irrelevant but the replacement-cost definition of value is irrelevant and resort must be had to other approaches. It will be suggested in Chapter Eleven that in such instances there is no effective substitute for present worth. With these exceptions, however, replacement cost has considerable theoretical validity because it approximates present worth.

The productive-capacity definition of capital also seems to be quite appropriate to the view of the contemporary corporation as a vital and continuing part of society. It is inconceivable at the present moment that organizations such as General Motors, General Electric, General Dynamics, General Foods, or General Mills, for example, are not a permanent part of the contemporary scene. Ownership may change but the organizations themselves will continue to pour out automobiles, toasters, airplanes, Jello and Wheaties; they will continue to provide thousands of jobs; they will pay taxes; they will make contributions to education and charity. Short of the extinction of or a sweeping change in American society, these and many others like them will continue because what they do is, in a sense, the lifeblood of that society. It is quite reasonable therefore to define their capital as the resources necessary to do these things; and since this view of capital is implemented by the use of replacement cost, the latter is an appropriate basis for accounting for the large modern corporation. The replacement value of its resources is an appropriate basis for appraising its status. If its continued operation is in the public interest, its capital can only be conceived of in terms of the money required to maintain that operation.

V

Acceptance of the productive-capacity view of capital and, thus, the use of replacement cost does not eliminate the need for the adjustment of dollar values to account for changes in purchasing power. The principal reason is that replacement cost is not relevant in the case of financial resources—cash, monetary investments, and receivables. In addition, purchasing-power adjustments may, on occasion, provide an administratively simple substitute for determination of replacement cost.

Changes in the general price level will, of course, be reflected in the changes in the price of any particular good or service and therefore replacement cost implicitly includes any changes in general price levels. However, one does not replace cash or securities or receivables in the sense that inventories or plant are replaced. That is, the face value of monetary resources would, at any given point, be replaced with exactly the same face value, and thus to state their replacement value is a meaningless act. (The *realizable* value of receivables, for example, may be less than their face value, but this is a different problem which can be taken care of by the traditional allowance for doubtful accounts.)

For the most part, cash and receivables turn over rapidly enough to keep more or less current with changes in the purchasing power of money. If monetary investments are in readily marketable securities, the current market price of the securities will probably discount whatever inflation has taken place while the securities have been held. If the monetary investments are not readily marketable, there is no such easy guide to their purchasing-power equivalent. However, unless monetary value has been absolutely stable during the accounting period, there will have been some change in the amount of monetary capital necessary to support a given level of these financial resources. The corporation's productive capacity depends as much on financial resources as on inventories and production equipment and therefore the monetary capital necessary to support the capacity should be shown. It will be fully shown only if corporation's capital is adjusted for changes in purchasing power of the resources held.

It should also be pointed out that only with such adjustments will the full result of the corporation's financial policy be made clear. For example, when the capital supporting certain resources is obtained through debt to be repaid during a period of inflation, the corporation will, in fact, have given up less purchasing power to acquire those resources than if it had paid for the resources with funds obtained from profitable operations in the past.

In Chapter Eight, the problem of determining replacement cost of fixed assets and the question of frequency of adjustment will be discussed. For the moment it is sufficient to suggest that the administrative problems of determining replacement cost each year may be substantial. In such a case, the adjustment of these values for changes in the general price level (which should be much easier to do) will take up much of the spread between historical cost and replacement cost. For relatively short periods of time adjusted historical cost will, in many cases, approximate replacement cost.

All resources are affected by inflation (or deflation) though the extent of the effect is in large part a function of the time over which the resource is held. Replacement cost (which includes the effect of changes in the general price level) is only relevant to certain resources, and practical considerations may preclude frequent adjustments to replacement cost. However, the total amount of monetary capital required to maintain the purchasing power of all of the corporation's resources is a vital fact about the corporation's status and progress, and adjustment of capital for changes in price levels must be made.

VI

The conventions of realized income and unrealized income are frequently encountered in accounting practice and literature. Essentially, the terms are intended to distinguish between increases in capital arising through sale of goods and services (realized income), and those related to resources still held (unrealized income). These conventions have not been considered here because they are relevant only if one defines capital and value, and thus income, in purely monetary terms.

If capital is thought of as a stock of competitive capacity, there will, of course, be changes in the monetary equivalent of the stock of capital. (The changes may, of course, be increases or decreases though only increases—the usual conditions today— will be considered here.) These monetary increments will appear in the corporation's statements and it is necessary to recognize that these amounts are not income nor are they increases in capital. They are nothing more than the monetary equivalents of an *existing* stock of competitive capacity. If the capital of the corporation (in competitive capacity) is to be maintained these monetary "increases" cannot, of course, be withdrawn without impairing capital. The "monetary" increase does not mean that the income of the corporation has increased. If capital and therefore cost are defined in terms of replacement cost, all income is realized.

Much the same can be said about the traditional distinction between income and capital gains. Increases in capital arising from the sale of the corporation's regular products and services are income. Increases in capital arising from the occasional sale of the corporation's productive facilities, for example, are capital gains. Such capital gains can only arise for two reasons: the corporation has resources not accounted for, or some of its resources are not properly (i.e., currently) valued. If resources were valued in terms of present worth, the latter type of capital gain would be virtually eliminated. The only time an asset could be sold for more than its present value to the holder would be when, for some reason or other, it would produce greater future receipts in the hands of another. To the extent that replacement cost is a reasonable substitute for present value, the same situation will exist. Capital gains arising from the sale of unrecorded assets are a different problem and suggestions for dealing with it are discussed in Chapter Eleven.

These matters will require a good deal of explaining, because they require a revision in the traditional way of thinking. In the broadest sense there are only two sources of capital, however capital is defined: investment from outside the corporation and from increases generated by the corporation. Thus, in the monetary view of these matters all money increases not accounted for by new investment arise from income or capital gains. It consequently becomes necessary to explain that with a different view of capital this generalization is not valid. Capital may not have increased; only the monetary equivalent has increased.

As stated in another connection, such problems must not be allowed to stand in the way of desirable change. There must be careful explanation by those preparing statements, and sincere effort to understand the explanation by those who read the statements. Unless one assumes these are possible, one assumes there can be no progress.

VII

The concept of capital as a stock of productive capacity quite easily shades over into what might be called the *competitive-capacity* view of capital. In this case, the corporation is viewed as having a certain position in its particular markets. Its capital is the monetary equivalent of the resources required to maintain that position, and it earns net income only after the costs of maintaining the position have been met from gross income. In a stable economy the competitive-capacity capital would be the same as the productive-capacity capital, but in a growing economy the former would provide not only for the replacement of existing productive capacity but for any additional resources required to maintain the company's competitive positions as well. Capital, in other words, would be the monetary equivalent of the corporation's stock of competitive capacity and no net income would be realized until the costs of anticipated growth had been met from realized gross income.

Historically, these costs of growth have been thought of as coming out of profits rather than as costs to be deducted before calculating profit. However, it is possible this is a matter of words only; that from the point of view of investors, management-directed reinvestment of profit is not, in a practical sense, profit at all. For example, in the steel-price controversy of April, 1962, the chairman of the United States Steel Corporation defended a proposed price increase as necessary "to help finance improved machinery, equipment and other productive facilities and research efforts, and to *arm the corporation to keep in the competitive race.*"[1] Since there is obviously no intention on the part of management in this case, and in most cases, to distribute at least a portion of so-called profits to shareholders, it is not unreasonable to label these sums as *de facto* costs, and to think of them as a permanent part of the corporation's capital.

(If the capital necessary to support growth is distributed as dividends, growth can only come by raising new capital. In the traditional view of these matters, it is generally maintained

---

[1]*New York Times*, April 22, 1962, p. 10f. Emphasis supplied.

that a corporation should "meet the test of the market" and raise new funds to finance growth. It is not generally held that new funds should be raised simply to maintain the *status quo*. If one thinks in terms of maintenance of present competitive position, growth is required to maintain the *status quo* of the individual corporation when the whole market is growing.)

Implementation of this definition of capital would be extremely difficult in many instances. There is no particular problem where commitments have already been made—as in the case of research programs and promotional campaigns. Where commitments related to necessary growth have not been made and when there are only plans to build factories or distribution systems, to increase working capital, to hire a new and more expensive but "growth-minded" president one obviously gets involved with a great deal of subjectivity and uncertainty. On the other hand, if growth is the foremost consideration of corporation managers, there is no denying the relevance of this view of capital nor the desirability of having such information available. Finding suitable means for doing thus must be high on the agenda of those concerned with accounting for the large modern corporation.

VIII

Before leaving the subject of capital and value it should be observed that in actual practice contemporary accounting procedures are a mèlange of all the views described here. LIFO-inventory valuation is a close approximation of replacement cost and thus of the productive-capacity concept of capital, though only in connection with income determination. The use of so-called accelerated depreciation is an attempt to account for income, in the short run, in the purchasing-power concept without actually adjusting monetary values. What has been called the competitive-capacity concept is not usually thought of as having a place in accounting, but surely many expenditures in research and development are made solely for the purpose of maintaining competitive position. Vast sums of money are knowingly and willingly spent on investigations which cannot possibly begin to yield net income until relatively far into the future. Many promotional expenditures and charitable donations also fall into this category. All these represent money spent today in order to enhance or protect the firm's competitive position in the future, and all these expenditures are normally deducted from current realized gross income in order to determine current net income.

It is true that these illustrations apply only to income determination, but this is only an indication of accounting's preoccupation with that phase of its total activity. The fact is that all these definitions of capital and value are used in contemporary accounting.

The use of replacement cost (as a practical substitute for the theoretically correct present worth) in measuring value would meet many requirements for accounting for the contemporary large corporation. It would eliminate most of the aberrations resulting from the changing value of money. It would give a reasonable measure of the extent to which the corporation has maintained its relative position, which seems to be what most managements are striving to do. It would divert attention from the largely irrelevant past and focus it on the present and, to a degree, the future. It would make the balance sheet a much more meaningful statement of the capital currently committed to the corporation and thus make possible a reasonable assessment of the effectiveness with which the capital is being employed. In short, it would provide, much more than does historical cost or a mèlange of widely differing definitions, a solid and useful basis for appraising the status and probable progress of the contemporary corporation.

Chapter Seven

INVENTORY ACCOUNTING[1]

I

During a period of time a business purchases or produces goods for sale, and in the typical situation some of those goods will have been sold during the period and others will still be held by the business at the end of the period. The essential accounting problem is the valuation of the goods manufactured or purchased. The value given to the goods still held is an important part of the corporation's capital. The value given to the goods sold is an important factor in the determination of income. Thus inventory accounting is an important element in all aspects of corporate financial reporting.

Inventory accounting illustrates virtually all of the problems and weaknesses of contemporary accounting. Because the accepted methods of inventory valuation are many and most varied, inventory accounting is an important cause of the lack of uniformity which so severely limits the utility of contemporary financial statements and reports. The almost exclusive attention given to income determination in recent years is vividly illustrated by the development of certain inventory-accounting techniques, and in no other instance are the frequently meaningless resource valuations which result from this exclusive attention to income more obvious.

---

[1]Most of the discussions in this book are relevant to all corporations. The material in this chapter is relevant only to those corporations engaged in buying or manufacturing and selling goods of one sort or another. Corporations providing financial or other services do not have inventories in the usual sense of the word.

It is important again to draw attention to the constant change which marks our recent decades and is implicit in all the discussions of this book. Virtually none of the problems of inventory accounting to be discussed would be problems in the event of prolonged and absolute economic stability; nor would they be problems if the nature and scope of the responsibilities and objectives of corporations were still as they were in the earlier days of the century. Since it is unlikely that we will achieve (indeed, that we want) economic stability and since it is certain that we cannot return to the age of normalcy, the changed and the changing must be accepted and inventory accounting designed to accommodate them.

II

For the most part, contemporary accounting for inventories is based on the monetary-cost view of capital or original-cost view of value. It is generally conceived of as a problem of accounting for the monetary cost of the resources (labor, material, services) expended during a period of time to acquire goods for sale.[2] The task of accounting is to divide the total pool of expended resources or costs between the acquisitions sold (cost of sales) and the acquisitions still held (inventory). A conflict between income determination and resource valuation is implicit in this procedure for if the accountant is primarily interested in income determination he will make his allocation of incurred costs in terms of achieving the "best" measurement of cost of sales and, from that, net income. Inventory value will be essentially the residual of incurred cost. On the other hand, if the accountant is concerned with the "best" inventory valuation, income will be the residual. (Given the emphasis on income determination, the latter situation is most unlikely to occur.)

In the first instance, of course, both inventory and cost of sales are based on quantities: quantities of goods held and quanti-

---

[2] For the sake of simplicity, the term "acquisition" will be used in the balance of this chapter to describe all goods—purchased or manufactured—made available for sale or for further processing.

ties of goods sold to customers. In a sense, the value of inventory and cost of sales are a function of these quantities, but whenever there has been a change or changes in the cost of acquiring the goods during the period, the cost to be allocated to each of the quantities remains to be determined. There are many methods for allocating acquisition cost to inventory and to cost of sales, but virtually all are variations on one of four basic procedures: specific identification; average cost; first-in, first-out (FIFO); last-in, first-out (LIFO).

Specific Identification

The obvious way of allocating the cost of acquisitions between cost of sales and inventory is by specific identification. That is, the cost of acquiring the specific goods held in inventory becomes the value of the inventory and the balance of total acquisition cost becomes cost of sales. However, except in retailing it is not common (and frequently not possible) to keep track of the actual costs of acquiring specific units in inventory. Consequently, specific identification is limited to situations where acquisition costs for specific items are recorded or can be traced back. Furthermore, because of income tax and other advantages arising from the use of other methods—particularly LIFO—specific identification is not necessarily used as a basis for inventory accounting even when it is practical to do so.

First-In, First-Out

The FIFO method of inventory accounting rests on the premise that the first unit acquired was the first one sold and, conversely, that the last unit acquired is held in inventory. The logic of the FIFO method is that it follows what is in a great majority of cases the actual movement of goods, for the oldest acquisitions are usually used first. It must be understood, however, that when FIFO is used for inventory accounting the first-in, first-out assumption is retained even if the actual flow of use differs.

In terms of cost, FIFO results in the most recent cost of acquisition being used as the value of inventory. Cost of sales is equal to the balance of incurred cost. (If all the inventory on hand exceeds the amount acquired at the most recent cost, the next most recent cost, and so on, would be used until all the inventory had been valued. (See Table A.) •

It is apparent that FIFO will in many instances result in an inventory valuation which will approximate current replacement cost. How close the approximation will be will depend on the rapidity with which costs change and the rapidity with which inventory turns over. In the illustration, the cost of acquisition is $200 at December 31, and so most of the inventory is valued at replacement cost. On the other hand, FIFO cost of sales will be different from the corporation's *current* acquisition cost. Again, the magnitude of the difference depends upon the re-

TABLE A

Illustration of Three Methods of Inventory Accounting

Part II of this table shows the calculation of inventory value, cost of sales and gross profit following the three methods of inventory accounting described in the text. The assumed facts on which all three calculations are based are given in Part I. The reader will observe that a steady increase in price levels is one of the assumed facts, a state which seems most relevant to our times. With decreasing price levels the differences in results would be the same, but the relationship among the methods reversed: that is, FIFO would yield the lowest inventory value, highest cost of sales, etc. Selling price is assumed to be a more or less constant markup on *current* acquisition costs.

I. Record of Inventory, Acquisitions and Sales for Year 19—.

		Quantity	Cost per Unit	Total Cost
On hand—Jan. 1		12,000	$150	$1,800,000
Acquisitions:				
From	*To*			
Jan. 1	Mar. 7	8,000	165	1,320,000
Mar. 8	May 24	14,000	170	2,380,000
May 25	Aug. 17	13,000	175	2,275,000
Aug. 18	Oct. 4	10,000	190	1,900,000
Oct. 5	Dec. 31	13,000	200	2,600,000
Sales		56,000	—	11,760,000 (selling price)
On hand		14,000	(see Part II)	

II. Inventory Value, Cost of Sales and Gross Profit for
Year Ending December 31, 19—

A. *First-In, First-Out*

Inventory

13,000 units x $200 =	$ 2,600,000
1,000 units x 190 =	190,000
14,000 units	= $ 2,790,000

Cost of Sales

12,000 units x $150 =	$ 1,800,000
8,000 units x 165 =	1,320,000
14,000 units x 170 =	2,380,000
13,000 units x 175 =	2,275,000
9,000 units x 190 =	1,710,000
Total	$ 9,485,000
Sales	11,760,000
Gross Profit	$ 2,275,000

C. *Last-In, First-Out*

Inventory

12,000 units x $150 =	$ 1,800,000
2,000 units x 165 =	330,000
14,000 units	= $ 2,130,000

Cost of Sales

6,000 units x $165 =	$ 990,000
14,000 units x 170 =	2,380,000
13,000 units x 175 =	2,275,000
10,000 units x 190 =	1,900,000
13,000 units x 200 =	2,600,000
Total	$10,145,000
Sales	11,760,000
Gross Profit	$ 1,615,000

B. *(Weighted) Average Cost*

Total Cost = 12,275,000 = $175.35 approximate average cost per unit
Total Units = 70,000

Inventory — 14,000 x $175.35 = $ 2,455,000 (approximate)

Cost of Sales — 56,000 x $175.35 = $ 9,770,000 (approximate)
Sales   11,760,000
Gross Profit — $ 1,990,000

D. *Summary*

	FIFO	Average	LIFO
Inventory	$2,790,000	$2,455,000	$ 2,130,000
Cost of Sales	$9,485,000	$9,770,000	$10,145,000
Gross Profit	$2,275,000	$1,990,000	$ 1,615,000

lationship between inventory-turnover rate and the rate of change in cost. It is obvious that the costs deducted from gross income are an understatement of the costs required to maintain the same quantity of inventory at current price levels of cost, and in this sense, then, FIFO results in an overstatement of net income. If all of the "net income" thus determined were distributed as taxes and dividends it is clear, all else being equal, that new capital from outside the corporation would be required to support the same level of inventory and operations.

Average Cost

The average-cost procedure is widely used in inventory accounting, probably because of its extreme simplicity and because of it sidesteps the necessity to make assumptions about the flow of goods. Basically, the method involves only determining the average cost per unit of all units acquired. This average cost is multiplied by the number of units sold and the number of units held to give cost of sales and inventory respectively. (See Table A). Usual practice involves a weighted average to take account of different quantities acquired at different costs, as is done in Table A. In some instances, a moving weighted average is computed, basically by recalculating the average at each new acquisition.

As is the case with most averages, the result is neither quite fish nor quite fowl. An inventory value computed from average costs will not, when acquisition costs have fluctuated, equal the current costs of the inventory. If costs have increased or decreased substantially over the period in question, the difference between current costs of acquisition and the cost of the inventory may be substantial. By the same token, the cost of sales will not represent the actual cost of acquisitions sold. The use of the moving-average technique will, in a period of changing acquisition costs, result in inventory value being more nearly equal to its current value, which is to say that it will approximate the FIFO method.

Last-In, First-Out

The LIFO method is in all respects the exact opposite of FIFO. The most recent acquisitions are assumed to have been sold and the first acquisitions (or more specifically, the inventory on hand when the corporation first adopted the LIFO method) are assumed to be always on hand. For the most part this is not the way in which goods are in fact consumed, though there are some instances, such as a pile of ore at a mine head or a pile of coal at a power plant, where the first material placed in storage may still be at the bottom of the pile.

LIFO results in a cost of sales which reflects most recent

costs. Thus LIFO tends to avoid any distribution as "net income" of capital required to maintain current inventory levels. How close LIFO cost of sales will be to the current cost of acquisition will depend on the relationship between the rates of inventory turnover and price-level changes. LIFO yields inventory values which bear little relationship to the present worth of the inventory. The longer the time between the adoption of LIFO and the calculation of inventory value the greater this difference will be, if price levels have changed steadily in the interim. In the illustration in Table A, LIFO inventory would, unless its quantity changed, remain at $2,130,000. If the upward trend of price levels continued it would be not many years before the then current value of the 14,000 units would be twice its accounting value.

LIFO and Income Taxation

There is probably no better illustration of the influence of income taxation on accounting procedures than that given by LIFO. In a period of rising prices it will most generally be advantageous to utilize the LIFO method in calculating taxable income for, as illustrated in Table A, it will result in a lower taxable income and therefore in lower taxes. When LIFO was first introduced into tax regulations in 1938 its use was permitted only by a narrow range of industries, but in 1939 it was made permissible for any taxpayer including, for example, retail stores where specific identification of goods can readily be made and where the pattern of use is definitely not last-in, first-out. Because of its obvious advantages to taxpayers during periods of rising prices it is not surprising that LIFO has been adopted by more and more companies—especially when the post-World War II inflation became apparent.

Tax regulations require that taxpayers using LIFO must also use it (and clearly state they are using it) in their regular financial statements. Thus the fact that the use of LIFO is quite widespread in corporate reporting is less an indication of its inherent soundness as an accounting procedure than of its efficacy as a tax minimizer. As suggested in an earlier chapter, taxation reflects responsibilities and objectives and procedural requirements of governments which have little relationship with the responsibilities and objectives and procedural requirements of individual corporations. Since it is these latter with which corporate accounting is concerned, it seems particularly unfortunate that regulations for determining taxable income should dictate the procedures of corporate accounting.

III

There are two obvious criticisms of contemporary inventory accounting. One is its extreme permissiveness. The second is that except in a time of absolute stability it simply will not permit achievement of a reasonably relevant statement of asset values and reasonably relevant statement of income.

No better example of the lack of uniformity discussed in Chapter Four can be found, for the wide range of "answers" made possible by conventional procedures to both inventory value and net income utterly destroys comparability. Furthermore, interpretation of financial statements is often made even more difficult because except in the case of LIFO it is not universal practice to indicate the method of accounting used. "Lower of cost or market" is not very revealing when several significantly different definitions of "cost" are possible.

It seems obvious, when alternate accounting methods are so very different, that there should be one method more nearly correct than others. In this case, none of the methods is right if one conceives of rightness in terms of current values. FIFO will be most nearly right in terms of inventory value. LIFO will be most nearly right in terms of income determination. Average cost will generally miss on both counts. The only effective way out of this dilemma is to discard the historical monetary-cost definition of capital and value as the basis for inventory accounting. The use of replacement cost, which is based upon the productive-capacity definition of capital and value, is the soundest basis for inventory accounting. Replacement cost will eliminate the effect of changing price levels on both inventory values and on cost of sales (income determination). It will indicate what an important resource is presently worth and will express income as a function of the current cost of maintaining that present worth.

For the most part, replacement cost should not be difficult to determine. Except in unusual cases such as tobacco, wine, distilled liquor and similar products whose production involves extensive aging, a current market price for raw materials and other purchased goods will exist. Current labor and other manufacturing costs are readily ascertainable.

The effect of the use of replacement cost in inventory accounting can only be compared with the effects of conventional methods if it is assumed that all the inventory is sold at one time on the last day of the year. Making this assumption, and using the data in Table A to illustrate, the following would be the facts. Current replacement value would be $200 per unit. Therefore, inventory value would be $2,800,000 (14,000 x $200) and cost of sales would equal $11,200,000 (56,000 x $200). Gross profit would equal $560,000. Reference to the summary of Table A will indicate that the difference between inventory on a replacement-cost basis and on the FIFO-cost basis is not great. On the other hand, LIFO cost of sales is the closest of the incurred-cost methods to cost of sales based on replacement cost. In contemplating these differences, the discussion in Chapter Six of the relationship between replacement cost and adjusted historical cost should be recalled. The acquisition costs given in Table A are in unadjusted historical dollars, and thus the difference between the several measures based on incurred cost and on replacement cost is greater than would be the case if dollars were adjusted for the decline in purchasing power.

Normally, of course, inventory is sold more or less regularly throughout the year. Consequently, the use of replacement value would require that cost of sales be based on current replacement cost at the time of sale. Practical considerations may require that adjustments of cost of sales to current replacement cost be made on, for example, a monthly basis, thus creating a possible small margin of error. It is also possible that with the use of modern electronic accounting machines, the adjustment at the time of sale may not, in fact, be impractical. If inventory were adjusted to replacement cost at the time of sale, the differences from FIFO inventory and LIFO gross profit would be less dramatic than these were in this somewhat artificial illustration. The important fact, of course, is that *both* inventory value and income would be on a current basis.

IV

The foregoing illustrates quite specifically the difference between the monetary and productive capacity definitions of capital and value. Conventional accounting rests on the assumption that inventory is really money and that if revenues exceed the money cost of inventory sold there is net income. Replacement value rests on the proposition that the inventory is part of the corporation's capacity to do business; that without maintaining a given level of inventory the corporation cannot maintain its position. Therefore, there is no net income until the cost of restoring the inventory sold has been met from revenues. LIFO is, of course, an attempt to define income in terms of competitive capacity while clinging to the words and symbols of original cost. It does not achieve this objective and further results in a completely irresponsible ignoring of the totally unrealistic resource values which result. A calculation of return on capital when LIFO has been used for some time will be grossly distorted.

Use of replacement value will, of course, require a "write up" of monetary capital to the extent that replacement cost exceeds original cost. As explained in Chapter Six, this does not mean that there has been a "capital gain" or that "unrealized income" has been recorded. Capital, in this instance, is units of inventory. If the monetary equivalent of that capital has increased, it simply means that the amount of money required to maintain the corporation's capital has increased. Neither income nor capital gain is involved. Nearly all contemporary financial reports of corporations refer, in one way or another, to "lower of cost or market" in connection with inventory. However stated, the phrase means that the inventory is valued at cost unless current selling price is lower in which case it is valued at that selling price. This rule of inventory accounting is basically a practical expression of the convention of conservatism and obviously conflicts with the convention of consistency. If inventory accounting is based on current replacement value, this rule becomes irrelevant because replacement cost cannot, by definition, exceed current market or selling price.

V

Virtually all management decisions about prices, changes in product lines, investments, etc. involve a comparison of expected gross income and expected cost. In these situations, modern management makes what can be called marginal or incremental analyses. That is, in approaching any one of the decisions mentioned, the usual questions asked are, in effect, by how much will the total gross income of the business change and by how much will the total costs of the business change as the result of a particular decision. A comparison of these changes, of course, gives the change in net income which is a basic factor in the decision.

The need to answer these questions has led to a great deal of study of cost behavior and to the breakdown of the total costs of a business into two broad categories: those which are basically a function of some particular activity and those which, in the short run, are basically a function of being in business. Material consumed in production is an example of the first category; ad valorem taxes on existing land and buildings illustrate the second. For purposes of this discussion, the first category will be called "activity costs," and the second, "time costs" (though this is done without prejudice to other names with which the reader may be familiar).

The traditional approach to inventory involves the inclusion of *all* costs of production incurred during a time period in the costs of the units produced. In essence *total* cost divided by *total* production equals unit cost. Cost of sales equals cost per unit multiplied by units sold and inventory equals cost per unit multiplied by units held. The use of FIFO, LIFO, etc. will complicate but not change the essence of this procedure which is that total cost of production will be equal to the unit cost of production multiplied by the number of units produced.

Under direct costing only activity costs are associated with units produced and all time costs are charged off as a total. Thus, cost of sales equals activity cost per unit multiplied by units sold *plus* all time costs incurred. Inventory equals activity cost per unit multiplied by units in inventory.

The difference between these approaches may be illustrated by reference to Chart A. The large square box represents total cost of production for the period which is divided horizontally to indicate activity costs (A) and time costs (T).

CHART A

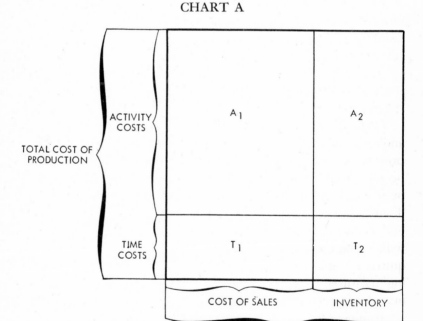

Under conventional cost accounting all costs would be allocated to units produced and therefore cost of sales would be equal to $A_1 + T_1$. Inventory would be equal to $A_2 + T_2$. Under direct costing, cost of sales would be equal to $A_1 + T_1 + T_2$ (T would not in fact be divided into T_1 and T_2) while inventory would be equal to A_2. This does not mean that direct cost of sales will always be greater than conventional cost of sales. The relationship, in any accounting period, will depend upon the relationship of T_2 costs of the previous period charged off in connection with inventory sold in the current period and T_2 costs of the current period. For example, in a period of very low production and relatively high sales following a period of high production and low sales, conventional cost of sales might well exceed direct cost of sales.

There is no question that for essentially short-run decisions about price, product lines, etc., direct costing is most appropriate since it focuses attention on those elements which will change as a result of a given decision. Traditional "fully allocated" unit costs are confusing and often misleading and the process of decision making has been greatly improved by the general acceptance of the idea of direct costing. This general acceptance has, in turn, led to constant demands for the use of the same basis for inventory accounting in published corporation reports and statements.

There is no necessary inconsistency between direct costing and the replacement-value basis for inventory accounting previously recommended. Replacement cost should by definition be equal to the actual outlays of resources which would have to be made at the present time in order to acquire goods for sale. Time costs will, by definition, be incurred in the short run under any circumstances and therefore the cost of replacement will be the cost resulting directly from whatever activity is required to replace the inventory. To the extent that direct costing measures these latter costs, it is an appropriate basis for inventory accounting in published statements.

It should be remembered that direct costing is only concerned with product costs. The issue is simply which of all of the costs incurred by a corporation will be included in product costs or defined as operating costs. Direct costing is based on the proposition that product costs are those costs which are directly incurred as a result of acquiring product. The essential soundness of this view is not affected by considering all costs as historical cost, current cost, or future cost.

VI

Inventory accounting illustrates many of the basic difficulties of contemporary accounting. LIFO is obviously an attempt to mitigate some of the effects of blind adherence to the monetary concept without departing from all of the other basic concepts. At the same time, LIFO well illustrates the overwhelming concern with income determination. The totally unrealistic resource values which it produces are generally ignored. Inventory accounting clearly illustrates the extent to which accounting is influenced by income-tax regulations.

The toleration of widely (one might almost say wildly) different procedures for dealing with a single problem clearly illustrates the extent to which accounting has failed to meet its responsibility to provide comparable and understandable data on which an evaluation of the status and progress of corporations can be based. The use of current replacement costs as the basis for valuing inventory on hand and for measuring cost of sales would go far toward providing data on the current status of corporations and on what resource commitments are involved in the maintenance of their position. It would further eliminate much of the confusion and ambiguity which surround conventional inventory accounting.

Chapter Eight

ACCOUNTING FOR
FIXED ASSETS

I

Accounting for machinery, buildings, land, and the other facilities in which and with which business is carried on is without doubt the most contentious and most discussed area of accounting. One would guess that the words devoted in books, articles, speeches, etc. to accounting for fixed assets, as these resources are commonly described, have over the years equaled the words devoted to all other accounting topics. This overwhelming attention undoubtedly occurs because fixed assets usually involve relatively vast sums of money which are committed for relatively long periods of time. Because of the length of these commitments, accounting for them is spread out over lengthy periods of time and thus becomes greatly affected by changing price levels, changing economic patterns, changes in technology, and changes in business objectives. Because large sums are involved, these changes often have significant effects on resource valuation and on income determination. Only the expert will get excited about accounting problems which, though intellectually challenging, involve only relatively minor amounts. When relatively large sums are involved even those with only a limited interest in corporations become involved.

Accounting for fixed assets is probably the most confused and confusing area of corporate accounting. A profusion of recognized accounting procedures yield widely different results. Terminology differs significantly from one corporation to another and is frequently quite unclear. The conflict between corporate accounting and income-tax calculation is nowhere more clear than in this area, and attempts to resolve it have given rise to new accounting problems. These same tax regulations have been a principal reason for the increasing tendency of corporations to lease rather than purchase fixed assets, and this has created new and unresolved accounting problems. The reluctance of accounting to change its procedures, to adopt a reasonable degree of uniformity, and above all to recognize that the great changes in the nature of corporate responsibilities and objectives require changes in the fundamental postulates about the role of accounting are most vividly illustrated by fixed-asset accounting.

The objective of fixed-asset accounting is the same as that of all other accounting: to provide the best possible information on which to base appraisals of the status and progress of corporations and to evaluate the extent to which they are meeting their apparent objectives. As suggested in earlier chapters, this objective is most likely achieved by attempting to state the monetary equivalent of the corporation's current productive capacity and by recognizing as income the residue of current revenue after this productive capacity has been restored. With these data it is possible to determine how much the productive capacity of the firm has grown. A reasonable measure of return on capital employed is also made possible, and this is a useful measure of the efficiency with which resources are being used. Finally, such data permit one to think about future prospects in terms of the current commitment of resources to the enterprise.

Fixed-asset accounting, however straightforward its objectives, is extremely troublesome because most fixed assets will be used by the corporation which has acquired them over relatively long periods of time—almost invariably far longer than the conventional one-year basis of accounting. While it is relatively easy, for example, to determine the *quantities* of goods acquired during a year which have been sold or are still held, it is often impossible to do so with fixed-asset acquisitions. What "quantity" of a foundry, for example, has been sold (used up) or is still held (available for future use) after a year has passed? It is this inevitable indefiniteness about some of the underlying phenomena being accounted for which gives fixed-asset accounting its somewhat special difficulty.

II

Choosing from among the several definitions of capital and value described in Chapter Six is the central problem of fixed-asset accounting. In considering this choice, it is useful to utilize Canning's definition of assets as "future services."[1] The buildings, machinery, equipment, etc. a corporation possesses are, in fact, the present material embodiment of future services. The assets are indeed goods, but the corporation owns them because of the service they will render in the future. Continued use of such an asset steadily reduces the amount of future service it represents. Thus the accounting problem is to state the future service potential represented by any particular asset, and to state as expense of any particular period the amount of service potential consumed in producing the revenue of the period.

Both these facts are ideally expressed in terms of present value. The *value* of future service potential is clearly reflected in the present value of the discounted future earnings estimated from the use of the resource. The cost associated with the use of the asset is the value consumed, which is equal to the change in present value during the period in question. However, as suggested in Chapter Six the procedural and conceptual difficulties involved in the implementation of present worth are, at present, too great to permit the use of present value in published financial reports.

Replacement cost seems to be a generally suitable substitute for present value in fixed-asset accounting. It is certainly a vast improvement over historical cost which in many cases will not even closely approximate the current value of future service potential, especially if an attempt is made to have costs include

---

[1] J. B. Canning, *The Economics of Accountancy* (New York: Ronald Press, 1929).

a reasonable estimation of service potential consumed. Replacement cost is an indication of value today, not the largely irrelevant past which is the basis for historical cost. If historical cost is adjusted for changes in price levels, the difference between it and replacement cost will usually not be great. However, the principal argument, stated earlier, for moving from adjusted original cost to replacement cost is that replacement cost is far more in keeping with the contemporary view of the corporation as an on-going instrument for the production of goods and services and the rewarding of those who provide its productive capacity. The importance of such an instrument lies in its capacity to produce both at present and on into the future, and a meaningful statement of the value of the productive capacity it currently holds must express the cost of maintaining it.

The substitution of replacement cost for historical monetary cost will require, as in the case of inventory accounting, an offsetting adjustment in the statement of the corporation's capital. If one accepts the concept of capital as productive capacity, the rationale for the adjustment is clear. At the same time, the conflict with traditional accounting usage must be recognized. All who have an interest in the distributable resources of the corporation must recognize that the increase (or decrease) is, *in effect,* an increase (or decrease) in the capital permanently invested in the corporation. It represents a change in the monetary cost of the corporation's productive resources. It does not involve an increase in distributable resources.

The use of replacement cost in fixed-asset accounting is unfortunately not so straightforward as it is in accounting for inventories. The relatively long service lives of fixed assets, rapid technological change, and their frequently highly specialized nature are factors which combine to make determination of replacement cost somewhat difficult. Broadly speaking, there are two approaches to determining replacement cost.

In some cases, replacement cost can be thought of as the current cost of an asset of the same age and in the same condition. To illustrate, the replacement cost, in 1962, of a 1960 model, two-ton Dodge truck would be equal to the current market price of a secondhand, 1960 model, two-ton Dodge truck in comparable condition. The cost associated with the use of the truck during any period of time would be equal to the decline in its replacement cost during that period. Actually, the case of automotive equipment is one of the few instances where the active secondhand market necessary to determine replacement cost in this manner actually exists. Consequently, its use is greatly restricted.

The other approach to determining replacement cost (which does not depend upon the existence of a secondhand market) is based upon replacement cost new less the decline in service potential since acquisition. In this case, the replacement cost of the two-ton Dodge truck in 1962 would be the cost of a 1962 model truck less the decline in service potential expected to accumulate over two years of use. The cost associated with the use of the vehicle during any period would be equal to the estimated decline in service potential. Implementation of this approach to replacement cost obviously involves (1) determination of replacement cost new and (2) estimation of the decline in the value of future service potential. These two problems are discussed in the following pages.

Replacement Cost

The most direct way of determining current replacement cost new is to utilize the current market price of comparable assets. For reasons given below there is no compelling necessity that the asset be an exact duplicate. Where this is possible, no further problems are encountered except for the matter of frequency of restatement also discussed below. In many cases, something more is required because changes in technology, design, processes, etc. have been of such magnitude that even approximate duplicates are not available. In such instances resort must be had to specialized indexes of labor and material costs from which the cost of replacing the asset today can be estimated. This is not the same as an over-all adjustment of accounts for changes in the purchasing power of money generally. Individual indexes of construction and manufacturing costs would include differences arising from changes in methods, procedures, etc., as well as those arising from changes in general price levels. This difference is an expression of the difference between the productive-capacity definition of capital and the monetary view of capital. The use of replacement cost is not a device for accounting for purchasing power expended. It is not an attempt to account for the current cost of some former investments in productive capacity. Rather it is an attempt to account for the current cost of the corporation's current productive capacity. That the several artifacts which are the embodiment of that capacity cannot be exactly duplicated is not relevant.

It must be acknowledged that the use of current replacement costs may, in some instances, involve an increase in current capacity. (The current model of a particular machine may have a higher output rating, for example.) In other words, the use of replacement cost may on occasion result in the inadvertent inclusion of costs of growth. This does not seem a serious matter when compared with the growth costs almost surely included in conventional accounting for research, promotion, contributions, and the like. And without doubt, carefully determined replacement costs will be much closer to current values than will historical cost.

The use of replacement costs involves consideration of the frequency of restatement to current replacement cost.[2] The task of determining current replacement cost of the thousands of individual assets controlled by a large corporation is a formidable one. (The general availability of high-speed computers may make it much less formidable. The Imperial Tobacco Company of Canada which restated its fixed assets on replacement

---

[2]See Robert Sprouse and Maurice Moonitz, *A Tentative Set of Broad Accounting Principles* (Accounting Research Report Number 3). (New York: American Institute of Certified Public Accountants, 1962.) This monograph came into my hands after most of the writing of this book was completed. While my statements do not always agree with those of Professors Sprouse and Moonitz, their views are close to mine on many matters, even though our work was quite independent. At this point, however, I must acknowledge a specific debt to them because in my original draft I had ignored the question of frequency of change in replacement costs.

cost in 1961 has said that the job was possible only because of computers.) If accounts are adjusted annually for changes in general price levels, there should be no need for such frequent adjustments of replacement cost. In general, the difference between adjusted historical cost and replacement cost should not be great until a few years have passed. Certainly, as Sprouse and Moonitz suggest, assets should be restated at replacement value whenever they are transferred from one owner to another. (See following chapter.) Beyond that, one can only suggest revision, say, every three to five years. Only careful study by individual companies will indicate where the spread between adjusted historical cost and replacement cost is great enough to require restatement to current replacement cost.

Decline in Value

The following discussion concerns the causes of decline, over time, of the future services represented by a fixed asset, the probable patterns of that decline, and the ways of accounting for it.

When a fixed asset is acquired it represents a stock of future services to the owning corporation. That stock of services is drawn upon as the asset is used and thus, as time passes, the stock of future services remaining grows even smaller. Since accounting must be based on monetary equivalents or values, it is most convenient to refer to this phenomenon as decline in value. Since the stock of future services declines over time, the value of the future services declines as well.

In estimating the decline in value of a fixed asset two elements are to be considered: the elapsed time until no value remains, and the pattern of the decline in value during that time. Each of these elements is a function of the underlying physical, economic, and social phenomena which are the basic causes of the decline in value.

Useful Life. The span of time over which the value of a fixed asset declines and disappears is usually referred to as its useful life or its economic life. The useful life of a fixed asset in the hands of a particular owner lasts as long as continued use of the fixed asset is more profitable than some alternative. Conversely, useful life ends when some alternative becomes more profitable than continued use of the fixed asset being considered.[3] Broadly speaking, this condition will result from one of three factors. In the first case, the fixed asset may have reached a physical state where it can no longer be made to operate satisfactorily or where the cost of doing so is higher than the operating costs plus capital costs of a replacement. The "wonderful one-hoss shay" is the extreme illustration of this. Secondly, the fixed asset may still function well but an alternative means for doing the same thing is available and the saving in operating costs is enough to justify purchase of the alternative means. Steam railroad locomotives—some of them nearly new—met this fate at the hands of diesel-electric locomotives in the late 1940's and early 1950's. Finally, the fixed asset in question may still be operable but the demand for what it produces has declined or disappeared. Many men's hat factories have become illustrations of this aspect of economic life. These second and third factors are usually lumped together under the single heading *obsolescence*.

Simply stated, then, the useful life of a fixed asset in the hands of its present owner is determined by the rate of physical deterioration of the fixed asset, by the rate of obsolescence of the fixed asset, or by the rate of obsolescence of the product or service in whose production the fixed asset is used. These rates of occurrence and the patterns they follow are the essential bases for measuring decline in value from which present value may be estimated.

The Pattern of Decline. Physical deterioration is constantly going on. In the case of buildings and other structures the mere passage of time with the attendant effects of change of season, etc. will bring about physical deterioration and use will, of course, add to it. Use is no doubt the basic cause of the decline

---

[3] The fixed asset itself may still have economic usefulness to some other owner; trolley cars sold by defunct North American street railways to South American operators, and Northern textile mills used as supermarkets, warehouses, electronics shops, and so on, are examples.

in value of machinery and equipment. Physical deterioration, whatever its cause, can be offset in substantial measure by repairs and maintenance, though there eventually comes a point where further repairs are not worth their cost.

The ravages of time generally become increasingly difficult to offset. The cost of restoring service value grows steadily and therefore the remaining value, in effect, becomes progressively less as time goes on. This means that value declines more rapidly in the early part of the life of an asset. Furthermore, there is a general tendency to use newer and more efficient equipment first, leaving older equipment to meet peaks in demand, for stand-by, etc. To the extent that deterioration follows use, the same pattern of greatest decline in early life should follow. Generalizations about physical deterioration are always subject to qualification, but surely it results in a decline in value which is progressive, the one-hoss shay notwithstanding, and which will typically be greatest in the early years of an asset's life.

Obsolescence is both progressive and sudden. Some obsolescence is always in the making as producers strive for marketable improvement in their products. Beyond this there is always a threat of sudden obsolescence as a result of new inventions or developments in the art or as a result of collapse in demand for the good or service produced by the fixed asset. The threat is there but the moment of occurrence, if any, is not known very far in advance. However, given present scope of industrial research and development with the resulting rapid changes in technology, and given the tremendous promotional and advertising efforts put forth to change consumer preferences, it is reasonable to assume that obsolescence will occur in a great many cases, that it will occur fairly suddenly, and that the likelihood of occurrence increases as the fixed asset gets older.

Recognition of Decline in Value. It can be concluded from the foregoing that the decline in value of fixed assets is inevitable, but that which has taken place and, more important, that which will take place cannot be measured with any great certainty. On the other hand, if accounting is to provide useful information about the status and probable future of the corporation it must provide fixed-asset valuations which recognize that decline in value has taken place and does take place. Furthermore, proper determination of net income requires a recognition that some portion of current gross income simply represents the conversion of fixed assets into goods and services which have in turn been converted into gross income through sales. This portion of gross income is a part of the capital of the corporation, and is not a part of net income.

The phenomenon of gradual decline in the value of fixed assets must be recognized. Since, in most cases, it cannot be recognized exactly as it occurs, the question is whether this recognition should be made in a fashion which conforms as closely as possible to the probable pattern of decline in value, or should simply be made in the most convenient way on the grounds that it will be inexact at best. Both points of view are represented by contemporary accounting practice.

(It is appropriate at this point in the discussion to recognize the term "depreciation" which is almost universally used in accounting to identify the process of accounting for the decline in value of fixed assets. It is unfortunate that the term is so used because it is widely misunderstood and the cause of much confusion. By definition, decline in value through physical deterioration and obsolescence is depreciation. Depreciation, as defined, cannot adequately be measured; it can only be approximated. The best that can be done is to estimate the extent to which the capital represented by fixed assets has been converted into other resources through manufacturing and sales. The use of a term such as "capital conversion" would not lead anyone to the conclusion that actual depreciation was, in fact, being measured.)

Depreciation Accounting

Current accounting practice is rather ambivalent on the matter of the extent to which the actual pattern of decline in value should be approximated. The definition of depreciation accounting of the AICPA can support almost any approach.

Depreciation accounting is a system of accounting which aims to distribute the cost or other basic value of tangible capital assets, less salvage (if any), over the estimated useful life of the unit (which may be a group of assets) in a systematic and rational manner. *Depreciation for the year* is the portion of the total charge under such a system that is allocated to the year. Although the allocation may properly take into account occurrences during the year, it is not intended to be a measurement of the effect of all such changes.[4]

This definition clearly states in its final clause that depreciation accounting does not attempt to measure the *actual* change in value which may have taken place, but gives little guidance as to whether or not it should attempt to approximate it. "Systematic and rational" can be interpreted in about any way one wishes. As the following descriptions of the principal methods of depreciation accounting in use suggest, "systematic and rational" does indeed mean all sorts of quite different things.

While the definition above refers to "cost or other basic value," contemporary accounting practice concerns itself with acquisition cost in virtually all cases. However, the methods of capital conversion or depreciation accounting for historical cost are equally relevant to accounting for fixed assets which are stated at historical cost adjusted for changes in purchasing power or at replacement cost. In what follows, it should be understood that "cost" refers to replacement cost. As mentioned earlier, there are at least ten systematic and rational manners described in various works on the subject. However, many of these are simply variations on the same basic idea or are used only rarely in very special situations. Only the three principal methods in fairly widespread use will be considered here.

Constant Deductions. By far the most common and the simplest method, usually called "straight line," is that which makes a fixed or constant annual deduction for depreciation or capital conversion. The procedure is extremely simple. Cost is divided by the estimated life of the fixed asset in years, the result being a fixed annual deduction. The net value of the fixed asset declines proportionately each year and the same deduction

---

[4] American Institute of Certified Public Accountants, Accounting Terminology Bulletin Number 1, Review and Resume (New York, 1961), paragraph 56.

is made from gross income each year. (The annual deduction is often referred to as a rate—10 per cent, 20 per cent, 12½ per cent, etc., but this is nothing more than presumably more convenient terminology. A 10 per cent rate simply refers to a ten-year life, etc.)

The constant-deduction method emphasizes the distinction between attempting to approximate actual decline in value of a fixed asset and simply making a "systematic" deduction to recognize capital conversion. The previous discussion of the likely pattern of decline in value suggested that it surely does not take place in equal annual decrements, and thus the fixed-amount method is not rational in terms of the decline in value of assets. By the same token, it does not satisfy the usual criteria for matching realized gross income and expense. The deduction for capital conversion will remain constant in the face of either lower or higher than normal volume of activity, which means that net income will fall more rapidly or rise more rapidly simply because of an *estimated* expense. Given the relationship between use and decline in value it is difficult to credit this procedure as rational. Indeed, its basic rationale seems to be that it gets done the job of making an annual provision for capital conversion in the simplest possible manner. Its operational convenience is no doubt the reason for its widespread use.

Variable Deductions. A number of related procedures, usually referred to as user or production methods, relate annual deductions to the actual use of the fixed assets. The pattern of deductions obviously varies with use. The methods differ mechanically from the constant-deduction procedure only in basing the estimate of useful life on output or machine hours rather than on time. Cost is divided by the estimated life in units of use, the result being a fixed deduction per unit of use. The annual deduction is equal to the product of the fixed deduction per unit and the actual units of use.

This procedure is often used in connection with transportation equipment, for example. The useful life of an intercity bus can readily be estimated in miles and the periodic deduction for capital conversion or depreciation based on miles traveled.

This procedure obviously cannot be used in connection with most buildings and structures or with any other fixed assets which do not have a readily recognizable measure of use.

If decline in value of future service potential is a function of use, this procedure, which relates accounting for decline in value to use, would seem to meet the requirement of rationality. If the estimate of the fixed asset's life in units is correct, this method would measure that aspect of decline in value precisely. On the other hand, it bears no relationship to the incidence of obsolescence and if the likelihood of obsolescence is at all great it will be an insufficient measure of decline in value. It is more efficacious than constant deductions in eliminating arbitrary fluctuations in net income. Since the annual deductions from realized gross revenue are a function of revenue (unless production and sales are not reasonably closely related) they should result, other costs not considered, in a more or less constant margin.

Compared with the constant-deduction method, basing deductions on use is more difficult. Records of use (machine hours, production, etc.) must be kept and calculations of the annual deduction must await the end of the accounting year. The constant annual deductions can be calculated in advance at the moment of acquisition of the fixed asset. Nevertheless, the production or user method is suitably systematic and by basing capital recovery or depreciation provisions on the use of the fixed asset it does have a recognizable rationale.

Decreasing Deductions. Several procedures for determining annual provisions for capital conversion or depreciation result in deductions of steadily decreasing size over the life of the fixed asset. Two different ways of achieving this effect are in general use.

The first of these, usually called declining balance or diminishing balance, involves the application of a fixed rate per year (typically twice the fixed-amount rate) to the unconverted balance of cost. That is, the previous year's decline in value is deducted from cost before calculation of the deduction for the present year. Given an asset with an estimated life of ten years and costing $1,000, the deduction in the first year would be $200 ($1,000 x 20 per cent). In the second year, it would be $160 ($1,000 — $200 × 20 per cent); in the third year, $128 ($800 — $160 × 20 per cent), and so on. A feature of this procedure is that the full amount of cost is never completely deducted since the unconverted balance will approach but not equal zero. Because of this, the expedient of changing from declining balance to straight line after half the estimated life of the fixed asset has expired is frequently adopted.

The second method is called "sum of the year's digits" and is simply an arithmetic device for obtaining successively smaller deductions. The annual deduction is a fraction of cost. The numerator of the fraction is the number of years of estimated life remaining at the beginning of the year; the denominator equals the sum of the number of years of estimated life. With a ten-year life the denominator would be $10 + 9 + - - - - +1 = 55$: 10/55 would be the fraction for the first year, 9/55 for the second year, 8/55 for the third year, and so on. A procedure which sounds so complex and has such a terrifying title should have some deep significance. "Sum of year's digits" has no significance other than resulting in successively smaller deductions, and doing so in a very arbitrary fashion, even though it appears quite scientific.

These two decreasing-deduction methods have had great vogue since 1954 when they were first permitted in the calculation of taxable income. There are other, perhaps more logical ways[5] of implementing the decreasing-deduction concept, but since these are the only ones permitted by the Internal Revenue Code, they are the only ones in frequent use. Prior to 1954, they were largely confined to accounting textbooks and examinations, probably because they are obviously more difficult to work with than is the fixed-amount method.

In the preceding discussion of the probable pattern of decline of fixed-asset values, it was pointed out that the greatest

---

[5]For an excellent and complete discussion of decreasing-amount deductions see Robert L. Dixon, "Decreasing Charge Depreciation—A Search for Logic," *The Accounting Review*, Vol. XXXV, No. 4 (October, 1960), pp. 590-97.

decline usually occurs in the early years of the fixed asset's life. The decreasing-deduction methods obviously reflect this pattern. Furthermore, since obsolescence is likely to occur before complete physical deterioration, and since the likelihood of obsolescence increases as the asset gets older, the decreasing deductions provide, quite incidentally, some hedge against both these possibilities. They do this, of course, by deducting the larger portion of cost during the early years of use. To the extent the new fixed assets are used more intensively, decreasing deductions should result in roughly the same pattern of deductions as those based on use. On the other hand, once the decreasing-deduction method has been put into effect the deductions are made annually according to schedule regardless of use.

The great appeal of these decreasing-deduction methods in this day and age is that they generally result in larger current deductions and thereby lower current taxable income and thus a deferment of taxes which would generally have to be paid currently if fixed deductions were taken. (Recognition of the greater value of the bird in hand plus a usual inability to stop hoping for lower taxes make the deferment attractive.) In a period of price stability and constant size for a corporation, these relatively larger deductions would eventually be canceled out and the "advantage" of the decreasing deductions lost. However, with continued price inflation and especially with continued growth, the canceling-out effect of lower deductions is regularly postponed. As long as the corporation each year adds more fixed assets than it retires, the deductions under the decreasing-deduction methods remain high because of the high deductions associated with newly acquired assets. If the corporation ceases to grow, the canceling-out process will eventually begin and if the corporation declines the process will be accelerated.

Summary. All the methods of accounting for the decline in value of fixed assets held by the corporation are systematic; whether they are all equally rational depends upon what one regards as rational. It seems reasonable to insist that a rational method is one related as closely as possible to the actual pattern of decline in value. In most cases the causes of decline in value of future service potential—physical deterioration, obsolescence of the fixed asset, obsolescence of the product or service produced by the asset—combine to form a pattern of sharp initial decline followed by progressively smaller declines. Obviously, the decreasing-deduction methods are the most faithful reflection of this pattern. (Whether either the declining-balance or sum-of-year's-digits procedures are logically rational or fortuitously so is a moot point.[6]) Deductions related to use are rational in those cases where sudden obsolescence is most unlikely to be an important factor. Where it is reasonably certain that useful life will be a function of use, employment of these methods is sound. The only rationale for the widespread use of the constant-deductions method appears to be simplicity. (One may suggest that general reluctance to change and the fact that a change to decreasing deductions from constant deductions would initially result in substantially lower net income are real, if not necessarily rational, reasons for continued use of constant deductions.) If one is primarily interested in income determination, this method does insure systematic deductions from realized gross income for capital conversion. It almost surely results in highly unrealistic resource values.

III

Fixed-asset accounting is no different from any other area of accounting in that it must be related to the role of the corporation in society. This role revolves around the capacity to produce goods and services and around the rewarding of those who provide the productive resources. Evaluation of performance in this role requires, therefore, information about the current value of the corporation's productive capacity, the resources required to maintain this capacity in the future, and the extent to which corporate operations are providing for the maintenance of that capacity and the rewarding of those who provide the productive

---

[6]*Ibid.*, p. 594.

resources. These broad requirements for accounting result in three specific requirements for fixed-asset accounting.

Maintenance of the corporation's productive capacity requires that the current cost of fixed-asset replacement should be the basis for accounting. Secondly, the current value of fixed assets in use must be known. Finally, the existence of net income should be dependent upon the cost of current replacement being available from realized gross income. These requirements are theoretically met by valuing fixed assets at current replacement cost less accumulated decline in value and deducting from realized gross income the annual change in the difference between these two.

Decline in value of future service potential is correctly measured by comparing the present value of discounted future earnings from future use of the fixed asset at two different points in time. The difference between these two present values is the true decline in that value. However, since this procedure cannot be implemented very satisfactorily at present, the more or less arbitrary procedure which provides for annual deductions of decreasing amounts should be used. It provides a reasonably accurate reflection of the typical pattern of true decline in value.

Once again, it must be recognized that when the replacement value of fixed assets increases there will be a corresponding increase in monetary capital, an increase which is neither capital gain nor unrealized income. Capital in this instance is productive capacity which has not increased. Only the amount of money required to maintain the corporation's capital has increased. Neither gain nor income is involved.

Both current replacement value of fixed assets and the decreasing-amount method of measuring decline in value are occasionally found in contemporary accounting. Unfortunately, many other procedures are also used and because of the large sums usually involved no better example of the deleterious effects of the extreme permissiveness of modern accounting can be found. For example, if a corporation acquired new fixed assets with a useful life of ten years at a cost of $10,000,000 during a year, the following accounting results (among many others) are possible. If constant deductions for decline in value were used, net income would be greater by $1,000,000 than if the declining-balance method were used. Also, at the end of that year the fixed assets would have an indicated current value of $9,000,000 in the first case and $8,000,000 in the second.

Many people who have an important interest in corporate affairs are quite likely unwittingly to make wrong decisions, if the decisions are based on income data subject to such capricious variation. They will be further misled by contemplating the probable future of corporations on the basis of the value of its resources. Clearly, the same resources at the same time, dedicated to the same use by the same corporation, cannot be worth $9,000,000 *and* $8,000,000. They must be worth $9,000,000 *or* $8,000,000 *or* some other amount.

Fixed-asset accounting involves the same conceptual and procedural problems as other areas of accounting. However, since the sums involved are relatively large and the time span relatively long, the need for resolution of these problems in accordance with the widespread responsibilities and present-day objectives of the corporation is nowhere more apparent.

IV

DEFERRED TAXES

Permitting the use of declining-balance or sum-of-year's-digits methods of providing for capital conversion for tax purposes has, when corporations have continued to use the straight-line method for corporate accounting, created an accounting problem of major dimension. The problem arises because the use of the different methods results in a difference between corporate income and taxable income in any particular year, even though the difference disappears over a period of time.

In Chapter Five, the question of the relationship between taxable income and corporate income was discussed and it was suggested there that taxable-income calculations should not influence corporate accounting. The problem being discussed here is somewhat different because the differences between the depreciation charges yield only temporary differences between taxable and corporate income. For example, the exclusion of dividends received from taxable income of corporations is a permanent exclusion (as long as tax regulations are not changed). The amount included in corporate income will never be included in taxable income. In the case of differing depreciation methods, the amount included in corporate income may, in any year, exceed or be less than the amount included in taxable income, but over the life of the asset the amount will be the same. (This assumes the same total amount being written off. If a corporation based its accounting on replacement cost while tax regulations permitted only historical cost there would be a permanent as well as a temporary difference.)

Before discussing the possible ways of accounting for this temporary difference between taxable and corporate income, it should be observed that the difference need not occur. That it does occur is a result of an apparent assumption that decreasing deductions for capital conversion are simply a tax "gimmick" and that fixed-amount deductions are in some way or other "right." Net income based on fixed-amount deductions is *correct* net income, it is assumed, while net income based on decreasing deductions is *incorrect*—an aberration tolerated for tax advantage. This assumption has no necessary validity because the decreasing-deduction procedures have long been recognized as "systematic and rational" for estimating decline in value of fixed assets. Furthermore, these methods are not "gimmicks" since more than other methods they reflect the probable pattern of actual decline in value. If decreasing-amount methods of capital conversion were used for corporate purposes, and they provide the most rational approach in a great many cases, the difference would largely disappear. It would not necessarily disappear entirely, because there is no reason to assume that rates permitted for tax purposes are necessarily the appropriate ones for corporate accounting. However, the differences might well be small enough to ignore.

Most, though not all, accountants[7] maintain that proper matching of income and expense requires deducting from corporate net income the tax which would have been levied at the going rate on that net income, even though the tax actually paid was substantially different. The difference between this theoretical tax and the actual tax paid would be added to a balance sheet account usually called "Deferred Income Taxes." In subsequent years when the actual tax would normally exceed the theoretical tax the difference would be deducted from "Deferred Income Taxes." In a completely stable situation where approximately the same monetary value of assets was being replaced each year, where tax rates were constant and there was no inflation, this account would eventually stabilize at a sum roughly equal to the difference between the actual tax and the theoretical tax in the first year. (Actually, the sum would not equal this amount unless depreciation already accumulated for tax purposes on assets held at the time the change over to the decreasing charge basis for tax purposes was made, were adjusted retroactively to the new basis and adjusted from taxable income in the first year.) If the corporation is growing, the balance of "Deferred Income Taxes" will grow, as it will with steady inflation. Deflation or a decline in the size of the corporation would have the opposite effect. If the corporation did not have taxable income in any year, the leveling off would not take place either.

For the most part, the arguments against this accounting procedure hang on the uncertainty that the theoretical conditions will ever be met. Future stability of tax rates, or for that matter of tax regulations, future stability of monetary value, absence of either growth or decline for the corporation in question are all required by the assumption that the "saving" in income taxes today will be offset by corresponding "losses" in the future. Some contend these are highly uncertain assumptions about the future.

---

[7]Ralph S. Johns, "Allocation of Income Taxes," *Journal of Accountancy*, Vol. 106, No. 3 (Sept. 1958), and Willard J. Graham, "Allocation of Income Taxes," *Journal of Accountancy*, Vol. 107, No. 1 (Jan. 1959). *Accounting Research Bulletin No. 44* (rev.) states the official position in favor.

The principal argument for deferred-tax accounting is based on the requirement for proper matching of income and expense. It is held that failure to state net income for the year after theoretical rather than actual taxes will overstate current net income on the one hand and not indicate that future net income, all else being equal, will be smaller. In other words, the deduction of an expense should be made from the revenue which resulted from the expense in accordance with the basic principle of accrual accounting.

Accounting for deferred taxes may be supported on grounds other than income determination, for failure to account for them is a failure to recognize a liability of the corporation. Because the difference between the taxable and corporate-before-tax incomes is only temporary, the tax is in fact deferred; it has not been avoided. Granted there is uncertainty, but the most likely thing is that it will have to be paid. Failure to recognize the liability, which means inclusion of the amount in net income, may result in the distribution, as dividends, of resources which will be needed to meet the liability in the future.

It is important that the amount of the liability for future taxes be constantly reviewed in light of current and expected future conditions. If deferred-tax accounting is approached solely as a matter of annual income determination, the liability becomes simply an aggregate of past annual deductions from income, and in that case the arguments against accounting for deferred taxes cited above may well have practical if not theoretical merit. Given this treatment, it is entirely possible that relatively huge paper liabilities will pile up; liabilities which because of changes in tax rates or regulations, because of continued growth, because of operating losses or changed replacement rates will not come due in the foreseeable future. It is true that failure of the expected liability to materialize does not change the total amount of capital held by the corporation, but it does involve a shift from capital provided in effect by the government to capital provided by profitable operations, and because it is on this latter that claims for dividends, wage increases, price decreases, etc. are based, it is important that the shift be recorded. Thus, the liability for deferred taxes should be reviewed annually and adjusted as necessary in light of changed conditions, past or current charges against income notwithstanding.

V

ACCOUNTING FOR LEASED FIXED ASSETS

American corporations have traditionally purchased most of the various facilities used in their operations, though some machinery and such things as office space in big city office buildings have been leased for use. These latter were leased because leasing was, for one reason or another, the only practical way of acquiring the needed facilities. Shoe machinery, for example, was until a recent court decision available only under lease. One obviously does not buy a fifty-floor office building to obtain a suite of offices. Except in these special cases, however, the almost universal procedures for acquiring fixed assets up to World War II was to purchase them outright with money borrowed for the purpose or with new or retained equity investment.

In the years following World War II, there has been a rapid growth of leasing—particularly the so-called sale and leaseback —as a major method of *financing* fixed-asset acquisitions. It is important that leasing in these cases is a form of financing rather than a necessary means of acquiring a particular facility. That is, there are no compelling reasons, other than financial ones, for leasing the fixed asset rather than purchasing outright.

There are many reasons for this spread of leasing, but the basic attraction is undoubtedly lower taxes. The rental payments are generally based on the return of investment plus interest to the lessor over a somewhat shorter period than the estimated useful life of the asset. Since, for tax purposes, the actual lease payments are a deductible cost, the taxpayer is in effect permitted a more rapid rate of capital conversion or depreciation than would be the case with owned assets. Furthermore, if the leased property includes land the lease payments will include the cost of the land, which means that the taxpayer is able to deduct an allowance for capital conversion in the case of land—something not permitted with owned land.[8]

Fixed assets may be leased directly from their owners who have acquired them in order to lease, as in the case of leases of fleets of automobiles, trucks, etc. Most generally, with buildings for example, the corporation constructs the building to its own specifications and sells it to some financial institution which immediately leases it back to the building corporation. The device of the dummy corporation is increasingly a feature of leasing. In this case the leasing corporation creates a dummy corporation whose sole function is to acquire property and lease it to the main corporation. The dummy corporation sells bonds to investors, bonds which are secured by the leases and interest in lease payments which it holds. The leases and related interests are assigned to a trustee by the dummy corporation who receives rental payments from the main corporation and makes the interest and sinking-fund payments on the dummy corporation's bonds. The common stock of the dummy corporation is entirely held by the leasing corporation, which means it controls the property after the bonds of the dummy have been retired and its leases reassigned by the trustee. Obviously this procedure is different only in its mechanics from the financing of fixed-asset purchases by a mortgage loan.

Virtually all leases are noncancellable during a period somewhat shorter than the useful life of the fixed asset. As mentioned earlier, the lease payments are designed to repay the lessors' capital plus interest over this same period of time. Usually the leasing corporation assumes responsibility for management of the property and all costs associated with it. Finally, there is a usual option to renew the lease or to repurchase at the expiration of the lease.

---

[8]For a full discussion of the advantages and disadvantages of leasing as well as all other aspects of the subject see the following, all in Volume 39 of the *Harvard Business Review:* Donald R. Gant, "Illusion in Leased Financing" (March-April, 1959); "From the Thoughtful Businessman" (July-August, 1959); Richard F. Vancil and Robert N. Anthony, "The Financial Community Looks at Leasing" (Nov.-Dec., 1959).

The Accounting Problems

The basic accounting problem results from the fact that traditional accounting principles provide no basis for the recognition of the resources held by lease. Ownership, the essential requirement for the accounting recognition of the existence of resources, is not present. Legal claims against the resources of the company, the traditional basis for the recognition of debts, do not exist. Under traditional procedures, the only recognition of the lease is the deduction of the annual rental payment from realized gross income as an expense of the year.

The important fact in connection with these leases is that, legalities of ownership notwithstanding, the corporation has basically unencumbered rights to use the fixed assets in question. An evaluation of corporate status and progress must be based on all the resources the corporation controls and on all the future commitments of resources resulting from that control. Assets acquired under long-term leases are, in fact, controlled by the corporation. Furthermore, since the fixed assets are presumably essential to the operation of the corporation, the lease payments are, in fact, future commitments, legalities notwithstanding. An adequate evaluation of a major oil company, for example, cannot be made if the information available does not include recognition of several thousand service stations and the current value of those service stations simply because the corporation has leased rather than purchased them. (The inadequacy is even more pronounced if the service stations are owned by a dummy corporation.) Neither the law nor accounting procedures, both exclusively concerned with the ownership interest, can be permitted to act as barriers to adequate disclosure of important facts about the corporation.

Many accountants have recognized this problem and recommend the inclusion, along with the corporation's owned fixed assets, of assets held under lease. It is generally recommended that the value of leased fixed assets be equal to the present value of future payments to be made under the lease, capitalized at a reasonable rate (the interest rate for the lease itself or an average rate for all leases). The same amount is also included among the corporation's long-term liabilities. Both these amounts would be reduced as rental payments are made. The theoretically correct procedure is to reduce the two amounts by the amount of the principal payment with the balance of the rental payment being deducted from realized gross income as interest paid.

Resolution of the problem of the dummy corporation is readily achieved by consolidation of its statements with those of its parent (e.g., the leasing corporation). With this procedure, no special accounting is required because the fixed assets would appear among consolidated fixed assets; the bonds would be included in consolidated debt; interest payments would be included in consolidated net income.

These procedures are quite commendable as far as they go, for they do solve the problem of disclosure of resources and obligations. However, these procedures are based on the premise that assets acquired under long-term leases are no different from assets acquired by outright purchase. Since this is so, all of the arguments given earlier for basing fixed-asset values on replacement cost are equally valid here. The fact that a part of the corporation's productive capacity is financed by lease does not (except for somewhat lower capital costs) diminish the capital required to maintain that productive capacity. Similarly, the arguments in favor of recognizing decline in value by provisions of decreasing amount are valid here. The fact that *financing* the acquisition of the right to use fixed assets involves repayment in equal installments does not change the basic pattern of decline in value of the fixed assets. (The fact that repayment is made over a period somewhat shorter than estimated useful life clearly makes the repayment schedule an inadequate reflection of the actual decline in value.) The use of lease payments as the basis of value of leased assets is a reflection of preoccupation with historical cost. The idea of insisting on the disclosure of leased fixed assets is essential, but the basis for doing so should be replacement cost less the best possible approximation of decline in value.

VI

ACCOUNTING FOR NATURAL RESOURCES

Included among the productive resources of many corporations are natural resources—base metals, coal, petroleum, minerals, etc.—which are not normally replaceable. In one sense these resources are like fixed assets from an accounting point of view, because the value of the supply declines as it is consumed and converted into realized gross income. Sound resource valuation requires recognition of the decline in value and sound income determination requires recognition of the capital conversion. The difference between these wasting or depletable resources and fixed assets is the fact that the former are not replaceable, which means that the concept of replacement cost has no significance.

Traditional accounting for these wasting resources is quite simple. The cost of the supply controlled—mine, well, quarry, etc.—is equal to the price paid for it if purchased, or to the costs of discovery and development when appropriate. The amount of the resource available from the supply controlled—tons, barrels, cubic yards, etc.—is estimated, and a cost per unit of the resource calculated. As the resource is used, the quantity extracted in a year is multiplied by this cost per unit and the resulting annual *depletion allowance* is deducted from the cost of the resource and, as a provision for capital conversion, from realized gross income.

The real value of natural resources, as of all other resources, is the present value of future earnings from their use, appropriately discounted. The price which happened to have been paid for them when they last changed hands will be a poor measure of present value unless the resources were acquired very recently. The costs of discovery and development will only by sheerest chance bear any relationship to present worth. Consequently, a complete and reliable accounting for natural resources held by a corporation should be based on present value. (Replacement cost obviously has no relevance in the case of wasting assets which are, by definition, irreplaceable.)

102

In general, the estimates of quantities of natural resources in a given source can be made quite accurately by geologists. Estimates of future earnings are subject to considerably more uncertainty because they depend on estimates of future prices, future costs, and especially the rate of use. Because most natural resources are for practical purposes imperishable, extraction can always await a satisfactory spread between selling price and extraction cost. Capped oil wells and closed coal mines all over North America are evidence of this fact. However, the determination of present value does depend on an estimate of the rate of extraction and sale, and such estimates are inevitably uncertain. If it is expected that a proven reserve of oil, for example, will be sold at a given margin over extraction costs in twenty years, the present value of the reserve would be quite different from that with extraction and sale taking place over thirty years.

On the other hand, the uncertainty involved in the estimate of the present worth of a supply of natural resources is more tolerable in terms of evaluation of corporate status and probable future than is the virtual assurance of being completely misled by values based on acquisition cost. For example, in 1956 the Gulf Oil Corporation sold its Canadian exploration and producing subsidiary to the British-American Oil Company, Ltd. (a Canadian company in which Gulf had an important interest). The value of the net assets of Canadian Gulf, much of which were oil and gas reserves valued at acquisition cost, was stated at Can. $55,000,000. The selling price of these net assets, based on the market price of British-American shares, was Can. $355,-000,000. This latter figure was based on an estimate of the present value of the proven reserves of oil and gas held by Canadian Gulf. The difference between this figure and acquisition cost shows the wide margin of error permissable in the estimate of present value before it can even begin to be as obviously wrong and misleading as is value based on acquisition cost.[9]

As in the cases of fixed assets and inventory, basing the values of these natural resources on present worth will require under

---

[9]British-American Oil Company, Ltd., "Annual Report for 1956."

the rules of double-entry bookkeeping an offsetting balance. As in these other cases, this is only a problem if one thinks of capital in purely monetary terms. In that case, the increase (or decrease) required to offset the increase (or decrease) in the present value of the resource will be considered as income (or loss) and taken to be available (if an increase) for distribution as dividends, wages, price cuts, etc. If one thinks of capital as the productive capacity of the corporation, this offsetting balance is simply a change in the monetary equivalent of that capital. It is the money required to maintain the existing capital of the corporation and there is no question of its being distributable income.

Summary

This chapter has been concerned with a number of somewhat different matters all having to do with resources which are held and used over fairly extensive periods of time and which typically involve relatively large sums of money. These two factors illustrate vividly the effects on accounting of changes in price levels, in economic conditions, in technology, in the responsibilities and objectives of corporations. A particular accounting process which began in, say, 1955, and is still going on in 1962, must be based on the premise that many conditions have changed and will change. Basically, it can avoid misleading only if it is related to current conditions and current plans for the future. Accounting based on historical cost may be of relevance to the ownership interest. It certainly results in values which have little relevance to the current value of the resources or to any of the other constituencies of the corporation.

The fact that large sums of money are usually involved in fixed assets magnifies the differences resulting from essentially free choice from among different and frequently conflicting accounting procedures. Accepted procedures for accounting for capital conversion completely destroy any comparability among the financial reports of corporations and in important degree make the process of valuation an exercise in futility.

Finally, the influence of essentially irrelevant factors such as income taxation and forms of financing is particularly evident in the case of fixed assets. That corporations pay income taxes and how they finance their productive resources are important facts which should be accounted for. They should not, however, be permitted to dictate the way in which resources held by the corporation and the uses of those resources are accounted for.

Fixed-asset accounting illustrates clearly the extent to which accounting is still conceived of in terms of the monetary interest of stockholders. In large measure, it continues to ignore the role of the corporation as one of holding, in the interests of virtually all of us, the capacity to produce needed goods and services.

Chapter Nine

COMPLEX BUSINESS COMBINATIONS

I

Virtually all our large corporations are a collection of smaller organizations with varying degrees of individual identity and importance. Broadly speaking, these combinations fall into one of two categories which might be labeled integrated or conglomerate. Corporate acquisitions of other enterprises used to be aimed almost entirely at the integration of the several elements of a production and distribution process under single management, or at essentially lateral expansion of the enterprise. United States Steel Corporation is an example of this sort of combination. In recent years, there has been a steady increase in the creation of conglomerate corporations whose *raison d'être* has little to do with production and distribution. Businesses which have a record of operating losses are eagerly bought up because these losses can, for tax purposes, be offset against the taxable income of the purchaser. Purchase of another, albeit unrelated, business is often the most direct route to that contemporary desideratum—growth. Businesses are sometimes bought simply to obtain the services of a president or other official. These conglomerate corporations have little beyond common ownership to bind them together. The Avco Corporation, for example, operates radio and television stations, makes agricultural machinery, and engages in missile and space research.

Whether the over-all combination is essentially integrated or a conglomerate of diverse activities, the smaller organizations making it up may exist in one of two ways. They may be simply operational units based on geographical separation, product differences, company administrative philosophy, and the like. In other cases, the individual organizations exist as separate and distinct legal entities. This may be so because of local company law or tax advantage. It may be so because inertia has kept from liquidation a previously acquired corporation. American Telephone and Telegraph Company is an example of a collection of separate corporate identities even though most of them do exactly the same thing and are collectively operated as a single business entity. General Motors Corporation, on the other hand, is (except for foreign subsidiaries) largely made up of nonincorporated operating divisions, even though the divisions may be as different in a business sense as are the locomotives, automobiles, waffle irons, etc. which they manufacture and sell.

Whatever the broad nature of the combination and however its several elements are organized, the existence of these complex corporations creates two largely contrary needs for information in appraising status and performance. There is a need for information about the over-all, essentially financial enterprise and a need for information about the individual business enterprises which make up the larger unit. Whatever the make-up of the corporation, the interest of the stockholder is essentially represented by the net resources of the over-all enterprise. Information relevant to this interest is in some degree provided by the traditional process of consolidating financial statements. These are discussed in the latter part of the chapter. Information about the parts of the combination is in many ways the antithesis of consolidation and is in the interest of virtually all of the corporation's constituencies. Its provision is discussed in the following pages.

II

For those who are not owners or top management but do have an interest in the affairs of the corporation, information about the over-all financial entity is important but information about the parts may be of equal importance. For example, the employee of a television or radio station of the Crosley Broadcasting Corporation, a wholly owned subsidiary of Avco Corporation, is no doubt far more concerned with the affairs of Crosley than he is with the New Idea Division of the corporation which makes agricultural machinery or the Avco-Everett Research Laboratory which is engaged in missile and space research. Since his own personal stake presumably lies in the future of the broadcasting company, his primary need for information in evaluating that future is information about the broadcasting company, not about the plow factory nor about the financial combination of television station, plow factory, and space-research laboratory.

Similarly, both customers and the public have an obvious need for information about, for example, the Electro-Motive Division of General Motors Corporation. This nonincorporated enterprise was largely responsible for developing the diesel-electric railroad locomotive and succeeded, in the ten years following World War II, in selling seven out of every ten locomotives in present use on American railroads. None outside of General Motors officials knows whether this division has been as successful financially as it has been in nearly monopolizing the railroad locomotive industry in the United States, yet for those who must evaluate the way corporations are meeting their widespread responsibilities this is vital information.

In terms of accounting and reporting, dealing with such situations involves some problems of accounting procedure, but essentially it is simply a matter of greater disclosure of relevant information. The accounting problem arises because the extent to which one division or subsidiary can be separated from other divisions or subsidiaries within the corporate complex is always problematical. In simple cases, the parent corporation provides some top-management service, including financing and perhaps legal services. In a more complex situation, divisions and even subsidiaries may share production facilities as well as management, legal, accounting, purchasing, advertising, selling, and other services. In the former case, it is relatively easy to isolate the relevant resources and costs and revenues of the enterprise in question; in the latter case, any separation is bound to be difficult and arbitrary at best.

Problems involved in accounting for the several parts of a greater whole are regularly faced in the preparation of data for internal management purposes. They are also generally encountered where foreign subsidiaries are involved, because statements of some sort for operations within a country are required by company law and tax regulations in nearly all countries. Subject to the qualifications set forth below, procedures followed in these cases are appropriate for the financial reporting of these complex corporations.

It seems appropriate that the sales of all of a corporation's major products or services should be disclosed. Other types of information, such as costs, net income, assets, etc., appear to be required only when the parts of the complex are significantly different. To use General Motors as an illustration once again, the Electro-Motive Division and the Frigidaire Division are each sufficiently different from the several automobile divisions to warrant fairly complete disclosure of their affairs. They do, after all, operate in industries quite different from the automobile industry, and there is no more reason to consider them in terms of the automobile industry than to think of the G.M. automobile divisions as a part of the home-appliance or locomotive industries. (It is, in a sense, only a matter of chance and definition that General Motors Corporation produces refrigerators rather than "Frigidaire Corporation" producing automobiles.) On the other hand, there seems no good reason for insisting on a separation of resources and expenses among the various automobile divisions of General Motors. It is presumably only a matter of administrative philosophy that inexpensive Pontiacs, for example, and expensive Chevrolets are manufactured by different divisions. Any arguments for separate reports on these divisions would be equally relevant for separate reports on each of the various brands, models, etc. within these divisions. Such procedures generally applied would mean, for example, that the H. J. Heinz Company would have to publish fifty-seven financial reports. Such reports would serve no useful nonmanagement purpose and because of the virtual impossibility of separating common facilities the task would be rather like trying to unscramble an egg—the results would be virtually meaningless.

Where significantly different businesses are held by common ownership, the possibility of presenting useful information about them is great simply because the businesses have so little in common. Common production facilities are unlikely. (One cannot make plows in a TV studio.) Common distribution systems are often not feasible because the markets are so different. Common legal and financial services are generally quite possible, and, of course, over-all direction of a single top management is implicit. These services are often paid for by an assessment against the subsidiaries, a procedure quite common in the case of foreign subsidiaries. This procedure is a suitable basis for financial reporting as long as the amount of the fees is disclosed. Some allocation of facilities might be required in some cases, but here again there should be no great problem in the use of such statements for evaluating the status and progress of the business if the basis of allocation is stated.

Summary. When a large corporation operates basically separate businesses, as is increasingly the case, there is a need on the part of all concerned for information relating to these essentially separate businesses. Whether the separate businesses are carried on by operating divisions or by legally distinct corporations is not, in this sense, important. Facts about significant parts of our economy should not be obscured by legal or operating procedures. While separate reports on these businesses will include some arbitrary items, disclosure of the basis on which the items are included should insure objectivity.

III

In the preceding pages, the necessity for what might be called the fragmentation of the reports of large, conglomerate corporations has been discussed. It was suggested in the introduction to this chapter that there is also a need for the combination or consolidation of the financial statements of separate corporations which are, in a practical sense, all of a piece. The American Telephone and Telegraph Company may again be used as an illustration, for it is only because of historical accident or state laws and regulations that there are several operating telephone companies within the Bell system. These operating telephone companies do the same thing and are, in fact, all a part of a national telephone system. To this extent, AT and T is a single business enterprise. (Some of its ancillary operations, such as its manufacturing subsidiary, Western Electric, are not necessarily a part of a telephone system.)

In such cases, there are no financial statements or reports relating to the over-all business enterprise and thus no useful basis for financial appraisal and evaluation of the enterprise by an outsider. This is so because the over-all entity has no existence in the legal sense, and accounting concerns itself with legal entities. In the traditional view, accounting is concerned with reporting on the sources and dispositions of property, and property must, by definition, belong to a person—real or legal. The business entity being discussed here does not have the legal status of person and thus has no property for which to account. The several parts of the entity own property; they have resources, capital, and income, and these are accounted for. The over-all financial entity does not.

Unfortunately, the statements of the several legal parts of the entity are not likely to be of much assistance in appraisal and evaluation of the over-all groups of companies. Two basic reasons for this, discussed in more detail below, are:

1. The resources, capital, and income of the holding company, shown on its financial statements, may be quite unrepresentative of the resources, capital, and income of the economic entity as a whole.

2. Analysis of the over-all entity through the separate statements of all of the organizations within the group is exceedingly complex, and perhaps impossible. In addition, the separate statements may, from the over-all point of view, be incorrect.

Holding-company Statements

In most situations, the equity securities of only the parent company are held outside the group of companies. In law, these securities represent ownership of the parent company alone. Indirectly, of course, through the parent company's ownership, they represent ownership of the subsidiary companies. In many groups of companies, however, the parent company is simply a holding company with actual operations being carried on by the subsidiaries. In such instances the resources, capital, and income of the parent company may have little relationship to those of the whole group of companies.

It is usual practice for a parent company to value its investment in a subsidiary at historical monetary cost. Dividends received from the subsidiary are included in the parent company's income, but undistributed earnings of the subsidiary are not added to the value of the investment. Thus unless all of the earnings of the subsidiary are paid out as dividends, the net resources of the subsidiary owned by the parent will be larger than the investment in the subsidiary as shown on the books of the parent company.

It is possible, of course, for the parent company to add to its investment account each year the undistributed earnings of the subsidiary company. A famous example of this practice has been the treatment by the Du Pont company of its investment in General Motors. (General Motors is not a subsidiary of Du Pont, but the latter has held approximately 22 per cent of General Motors stock since that company's founding.) Each year Du Pont has adjusted its "Investment in General Motors" account to equal its proportionate share in the net assets of General Motors. The necessary write-up or write-down from the previous year's balance has been shown in the Du Pont income statement.

This procedure has generally been frowned upon by accountants because it departs from the historical-cost basis for accounting and involves a so-called unrealized gain. Actually, the arguments made in other connections for stating current values of all resources and the monetary equivalents of the capital required to maintain the productive capacity of the corporation are equally valid here. The current value of the net resources of the subsidiary (assuming its resources are adequately valued) are in all significant ways part of the value of the resources of the parent corporation. The form of ownership is different but its substance is that of direct ownership of the individual resources by the parent corporation. There seems no reason, other than the narrowly legalistic one, for not showing investment in subsidiary companies at its current value.

Even if the foregoing were accepted procedure, however, the need for consolidated financial statements would not be eliminated. The parent or holding-company statement would show the current value of the subsidiary, but only in the aggregate. Important information about the resources and the sources of the capital of the over-all organization would be buried in a most uninformative "Investment in Subsidiary Company" account. Nor would presentation of separate statements for the parent corporation and each subsidiary, in most cases, provide a workable solution to the problem of evaluating the enterprise as a whole.

In the first place, if the enterprise consists of dozens of separate companies, which is not uncommon, or even of only five or six companies, it is practically impossible for even an expert to visualize the over-all situation.

In the second place, the resources, capital, and income of the individual companies may be seriously overstated in terms of the total enterprise to the extent that transactions among the companies are included. A debt of one subsidiary company to another is in all ways a legitimate asset of the creditor company, but in terms of the total enterprise the debt has no more economic significance than would debts of one department to another in a single corporation. The same is true of purchases and sales among associated companies, which are appropriately a part of the purchases or sales of the companies themselves but are irrelevant in terms of the total enterprise. Without information about such intercompany transactions included in the resources, capital, and income of the individual companies of a group of companies, their individual statements cannot be relied upon to give a reasonable picture of the total enterprise.

In order to overcome these several difficulties and to make it possible to present a statement of the financial and operating affairs of an economic entity, the device of consolidated financial statements has been developed. Such statements consolidate or put together the statements of the separate companies and approximate the financial statements which would exist if the entire enterprise were operated under a single corporate structure.

Basically, the consolidation of financial statements involves canceling out or eliminating transactions between the companies whose statements are being consolidated. An illustration may be based on a sale, for credit, by Company A to Company B. This transaction involves a sale and an account receivable for A, a purchase and an account payable for B. In consolidation of the statements of A and B the receivable of A and the payable of B would be canceled out on the grounds that in terms of the economic entity the obligation is of itself and to itself. The revenue from the sale recorded by A and the cost of the sale recorded by B would also be eliminated since for the economic entity the sale is, in effect, by itself to itself.

There may be many difficult operational problems involved in consolidating financial statements, but for the most part these do not affect the substance and meaning of the results. More important is the subjective question of when consolidation of financial statements should be undertaken. This is considered in the following section.

Conditions for Consolidation

It has already been said that the purpose of consolidation statements is to portray the financial results of the operations of an economic entity not represented by a corresponding legal entity. The idea of an economic entity implies control of its assets, including freedom to shift assets within the enterprise. The idea also implies some degree of similarity among the several parts of the entity. Because of these implications, a number of

114

considerations are involved both in a decision to present consolidated financial statements and in the interpretation of such statements.

Ownership. Control of assets is basically a function of ownership and thus the extent of ownership of the equity of subsidiary companies becomes a governing factor in consolidations. Probably the vast majority of subsidiary companies are entirely owned by the parent organization. There are, however, many partially owned subsidiaries, usually those which have been purchased as going concerns. Thus it becomes necessary to consider the extent of ownership of a subsidiary, which should be prerequisite to including it in a consolidation.

Many companies follow the rule of consolidating only those subsidiaries which are 100 per cent owned. Such a rule leaves no doubt about the question of control, though it does not guarantee freedom to shift assets within the enterprise. It also has the virtue of simplicity because it eliminates the necessity for indicating the minority interest which is involved when partially owned subsidiaries are consolidated. (See below.)

On the other hand, this rule may not result in a presentation of the financial results of operations of a *de facto* economic entity, because control of assets may exist even when ownership is not complete. While a minority shareholder has some legal "rights," these are generally not strong enough to prevent an action of the majority. For this reason, some companies follow the rule of consolidating the assets, liabilities, and profits of all subsidiary companies of which they own in excess of 50 per cent. Between 50 per cent ownership and complete ownership there is, of course, a great variety of possible ownership levels which may be considered as representing effective control.[1]

---

[1] When partially owned subsidiaries are included in consolidated statements, some modification of the statements is required. It is usual practice to include all of the resources of all of the corporations in the consolidation but to indicate that they are not entirely owned by the consolidated group by indicating the amount of the minority interest. (In general this is equal to the par or stated value of the stock held plus a pro rata share of retained earnings.) This amount is neither a liability of the consolidation nor a part of its equity. It is usually labeled "Minority Interest in Subsidiary Company" and listed after the consolidated liabilities and before consolidated equity.

Similarity. In many instances, one company may have complete ownership of another company without there being a sound basis for consolidation of financial statements. This would be the case in situations where the owned and owning companies are engaged in totally different types of business and thus the economic entity which consolidated statements are intended to represent does not exist. For example, a bank, as a result of the default of a debtor, might find itself the sole owner of a spaghetti factory. Few would argue that banking and spaghetti making form an economic entity. Because of this lack of similarity, the American Telephone and Telegraph Company does not include in the consolidated statements of the group of operating telephone companies the accounts of Western Electric Company, its manufacturing subsidiary, which is almost entirely owned by American Telephone. For similar reasons, General Motors consolidates the accounts of its many manufacturing subsidiaries but excludes the wholly owned General Motors Acceptance Corporation, which is a finance company.

In this area, as in the case of ownership, decisions are inevitably subjective. There can be no hard and fast rules as to what constitutes an economic entity. General Motors considers the manufacture of automobiles, railway locomotives, and household appliances as an economic entity. Some other company might consider waffle irons and Cadillacs quite unrelated.

Foreign Subsidiaries. The existence of foreign subsidiaries poses some particular problems in terms of consolidated financial statements. Ownership of a foreign subsidiary may be complete and it may be in exactly the same business as the home-country parent yet, because of exchange controls, freedom to shift assets within the entity may not exist. Some countries may have accounting and fiscal regulations which make the statements of a company in that country quite noncomparable with those in other countries. Consolidation also creates problems of currency conversion, since consolidated statements can have meaning only when stated in a single currency. If the value of one currency fluctuates in terms of the other, should one use values at statement date, average rate, year-end rate, etc.? More broadly, does

116

a consolidated statement of assets based on hard currencies with assets based on currencies subject to extreme inflation have any practical significance? Once again, answers to these questions must be highly subjective.

The objective in consolidating financial statements is to go beyond essentially artificial legal barriers and try to present fairly the financial status of an economic entity. In order to do this one must have some criteria by which the existence of an economic entity can be established. Such criteria are embodied in the questions just discussed: degree of ownership, extent of control over resources, nature of businesses, etc. Generally speaking, there can be no hard and fast rules about these matters and each case must be decided on its own merits. Furthermore, these questions become less critical if consolidation is not thought of in all-or-nothing terms, if the need to disclose significant information is not lost sight of in concern for the process of consolidation. It may be stated again that consolidation is a useful way of indicating the interest of stockholders. In the case of a group of companies representing a basically unified production and distribution process, consolidated statements may reveal other important information as well. In the case of conglomerate combinations consolidated statements obscure more than they reveal—except about the stockholder interest. Thus if one accepts the necessity for disclosing all relevant information about the parts of the whole as well as about the consolidated whole, the several criteria for consolidation become of less importance.

IV

One further aspect of consolidated financial statements arises because the price paid by one corporation when purchasing another is rarely equal to the accounting value of the purchased company. (For the sake of simplicity, the situation will be discussed where price paid exceeds the accounting value. This seems the more usual situation, though the reverse can be and sometimes is true. The basic problem is the same in either case.)

Broadly speaking, this situation results from a combination of two facts: recorded assets of the purchased company are undervalued or some of its assets are not recorded at all. Put another way, the price paid for a going business is presumably related to the current market value of that business which is, in turn, a function of the present value of the future earnings of its resources. Such values are almost never reflected in a corporation's accounts.

As far as the purchasing company is concerned, the value of its investment is, at the time of purchase, the amount paid for the other business. (The cost is obvious if the purchase price is paid in cash. If, as is frequently the case, it is paid for in the stock of the purchasing company, some complications may arise. However, as long as the stock of the purchasing company has a recognized market value—and in the case of the large corporations with which we are concerned, this will virtually always be so—this market value obviously represents the price paid.) Thus, the equity in the purchased company, based on the price paid for its shares, will appear in the accounts and statements of the purchasing company at a higher amount than the amount of the equity as shown in the accounts and statements of the purchased company. This discrepancy is not apparent until one consolidates the statements of the two corporations, but then it will be impossible to eliminate the entire investment of the parent corporation against the equity of the subsidiary.

These are recognized accounting procedures for dealing with this excess of investment over book value of a subsidiary company:

1. To carry the amount on the consolidated statement as a so-called intangible asset under some such heading as "Good Will Arising from Consolidation."
2. To allocate the amount to various individual assets.
3. To write off the amount against consolidated retained earnings.

In my view, the latter has no validity. The purchase of the subsidiary by another surely establishes the value of its aggregate resources and it is contrary to the basic objective of disclosure of all resources to write off the amount. If the excess arises because the subsidiary's listed assets are undervalued, the amount should be added to the value of these assets and thus appear in the consolidated statement. If the excess arises because some of the subsidiary's assets (probably intangible assets) are not listed at all, these resources should be described and listed. (This matter is discussed in Chapter Eleven.)

If accounting is based on current values rather than historical monetary values, this problem will arise must less frequently. In such cases their book value would be approximately equal to current value which means book value would be close to the purchase price. (It is unlikely the two would be exactly the same, because the net resources of a subsidiary would probably have a different value as a part of a combined enterprise.) The important thing, however, is that the value of resources is established at the time of the purchase of the subsidiary and if recorded values are different the latter should be changed. The difference should not be written off. The value established by purchase is not, of course, good for all time, and should be changed as the value of the resources involved changes.

V

Accounting for Mergers

The foregoing discussion was related to the consolidation of the statements of legally separate companies which are in other than legal respects parts of a single business enterprise. In many situations it will be expedient to do away with the legal distinctions too, and merge the purchased company into the purchasing company. This would always happen when a business's assets, rather than its stock, were purchased.

In the case of a merger, the accounting and reporting problems, considered from the point of view of the interested outsider, are little different from those already discussed. It is important that necessary information about a significant business enterprise not be lost. If the purchased company and its affairs are important to workers, to customers, to suppliers, to the public generally, the fact that it no longer has an independent legal identity should not be allowed to stand in the way of continued availability of information about its status and progress.

The valuation of the acquired assets involves the same problems discussed elsewhere. The important thing here is that the price paid for the net resources of the company presumably establishes the present value of the net resources at the time of purchase, and therefore that value should be used in accounts and reports.

Pooling of Interests

In recent years, accounting has given acceptance to a procedure which arises from the proposition that many business combinations are not, in fact, the sale of one business to another but are simply a pooling of interests by the owners of the two enterprises. The distinction between a purchase and a pooling of interests is spelled out in substantial detail in *Accounting Research Bulletin No. 48* of the American Institute of CPA's. In essence, a pooling of interests is recognized when the ownership interest in the assets of the several corporations is not changed by the combination of the businesses. The maintenance of substantially the same proportionate interest and voting rights is required. The continuation of all the elements of the business and the continuation of the control of the previous managements are similarly required. Put in the opposite way, there would be a purchase rather than pooling of interest when the ownership interests or proportionate control of any of the owners is eliminated or substantially changed; if a significant part of the business is abandoned or sold; if any of the control or influence of any of the previous management is eliminated.

The essential accounting distinction involved in a pooling of interests is that no new basis for accountability arises whether the individual companies retain their identity, are merged into one of the companies, or all disappear into an entirely new company. In a merger, the net assets of the purchased company would be added to those of the purchasing company. The capital and retained earnings of the purchased company would disappear. If the net resources of the purchased company were acquired at greater or less than their book values, their value would presumably be adjusted to the new values. In a pooling of interests neither of these would happen. The assets, liabilities, capital, and retained earnings of the pooled companies would be taken at their book values and simply added together. In the case of merger the equity of the surviving company would be equal to the equity of the purchasing company, plus or minus any change in the value of the assets of the purchased company. In a pooling of interests, the equity of the surviving company would be equal to the total equity of the pooled companies without any change in the value of combined resources.

When companies which have been pooled retain their corporate identities (for the same reasons that any subsidiary companies are kept as legal entities) it will usually be desirable to publish combined or, in effect, consolidated financial statements. The differences between such statements and those described earlier would be that the equities of the pooled companies would make up the combined equities and there would be no excess of investment over assets or excess of assets over investment.

The principal practical reason for following the pooling-of-interests approach, rather than the traditional merger, is that the retained earnings, and therefore the dividend-paying capacity of the combined enterprise, are not reduced. In a merger, the retained earnings of the merged company disappear, and thus the dividends that may legally be paid are reduced by the amount of the retained earnings. If the transaction is, in fact, a pooling of interests, there seems no good reason why it should not be accounted for in this way. A clearer statement of facts is given and no accounting artificialities are introduced.

On the other hand, the pooling-of-interests approach may mean a continuation of unrealistic accounting valuations by not making it necessary to face up to the actual existence of more realistic values. This is not, it should be added, a fault of the pooling-of-interest approach per se. If meaningless accounting values exist, they exist because of the accounting procedures followed by the individual companies. However, in the case of a merger or in the consolidation of financial statements of corporate subsidiaries, inadequate accounting valuations of the resources of at least one of the companies must be faced up to.

VI

Increasingly, the business of the nation is carried on by large, conglomerate corporations which have, in many cases, gathered a wide variety of businesses under a single financial roof. In other cases, an essentially integrated business may be fragmented among a number of legally separate corporations. These facts create two problems in terms of the evaluation of large corporations by those to whom the corporations have responsibility. In the first place, information about broadly important and essentially distinct enterprises must not be obscured by the fact of common ownership. Common ownership is relevant only to the ownership interest and, in part, to the management interest. For some of the other interests it is most irrelevant.

In the second place, the existence of separate legal entities must not result in sight being lost of *de facto* business enterprise. It is particularly important for the ownership interest that the business and ownership entity be reported upon.

Thus, the existence of large and sometimes conglomerate enterprises calls for both combination and fragmentation in accounting reports. Each of these will reveal facts and relationships essential to the evaluation of the way in which corporations are meeting their widespread responsibilities.

Chapter Ten

COMPENSATION

I

Two accoutrements of the contemporary corporation are the pension plan and the stock option. They are obviously responses to high rates of personal-income taxation for both provide the employee with a certain amount of low-tax or tax-free income. They are also, however, manifestations of the scope of present-day corporate responsibilities for they are based on some idea of responsibility for the relative welfare of employees—including management. Since both these procedures involve a type of compensation in the future for services rendered in the past, at present, and in the future, they are vivid illustrations of the inadequacy of the short-run, "as-of-now" view of the corporation. Implicit in both is the idea that the corporation will continue to exist far into an indefinite future.

From the point of view of accounting, these methods of compensation raise two questions. In the first place, they emphasize the need for basing accounting principles and procedures on more than the ownership interest. Owners obviously have an interest in compensation, because it directly affects their own potential share of corporate resources. Employees have a manifest interest in compensation and especially in the provisions made for promised future compensation. In the case of both pensions and stock options, but especially the latter, there are some important questions of the broad public interest. Consequently, accounting for these procedures must be oriented to the requirements of all the constituencies of the corporation.

The second accounting question is indefiniteness. At the

time pension and stock-option arrangements are entered into there is no definite and readily ascertainable cost, nor is their duration definite or even reasonably certain. Thus two of the main props of traditional accounting procedure are missing. Their absence creates no unsolvable problems but it does require a willingness to accept accounting methods which are different and which yield only uncertain results. The first part of this chapter is devoted to pension plans, and the second to stock options. It should be borne in mind that both of these are discussed here only in terms of accounting. Many economic, social, even political problems associated with these forms of compensation of corporate employees and managers are beyond the scope of this work.

II
ACCOUNTING FOR PENSION PLANS

There is probably no better illustration of the present-day scope of corporate responsibilities than the rapid spread of pensions for retired employees, largely paid for by employers. This is not to say that the initiation of pension plans is solely a response by corporation managers to moral or compassionate considerations (or to selfish ones for that matter, since managers themselves are liberally pensioned). Undoubtedly the combination of high profits and favorable tax treatment of contributions to pension funds has been a factor in their growth. Certainly there is a competitive aspect to pensions, too, for they are an important factor in recruiting and retaining personnel. Probably the greatest pressure has come from general public acceptance of the idea of pensions, which has been a response, in part at least, to the ever-increasing proportion of aged in the population. However mixed the motives, the adoption of pension plans is a concrete manifestation of responsibility to employees—including the members of the management group.

The existence of pension plans also implies the long-run, on-going view of the corporation. While no pension plan is set up in perpetuity, one is by its very nature inconsistent with the short-run view of the corporation since it creates a *de facto* obligation of generally indeterminate amount which stretches far into an indeterminate future. Pension plans clearly assume the pensioning corporation will exist for a very long time.

In the following paragraphs the basic characteristics of contemporary pension plans are briefly described. The purpose of these paragraphs is simply to sketch those characteristics which influence accounting and thus they are in no sense concerned with the multitude of variations found in pension plans nor with the many financial, economic, and social ramifications of these plans.[1]

Basic Characteristics

Duration. Most corporation pension plans are provided for in employment contracts or agreements—individual or collective —and the contract or agreement is for a limited time, subject to termination and modification at the expiration of such a period of time by management of the corporation. It is quite understandable that the contractual or understood basis for such plans would include provision for termination and modification on the grounds of ordinary prudence if nothing else. On the other hand, it seems eminently reasonable to accept as highly probable the relative permanence of pension plans. Internal Revenue Service regulations governing the deductibility of employer contributions to pension funds have tended to make the plans, in fact, permanent.[2] Perhaps of even greater importance is the simple fact that the idea of a pension has become such an important part of our socioeconomic structure. Pension plans have come to be considered the right of the employee rather than the option of the employer to such a degree that the relative permanence of pension plans seems far more certain than does arbitrary abandonment by management.

---

[1] Excellent coverage of all aspects of pension plans is found in Don M. McGill (ed.), *Pensions and Trends* (published for the S. S. Huebner Foundation for Insurance Education) (Homewood, Ill.: Richard D. Irwin, Inc., 1955).

[2] *Ibid.*, p. 76.

Benefits. Benefits under most contemporary pension plans fall into one of two broad categories. The first of these is the so-called money-purchase plan under which the corporation's annual payments into the fund are fixed and the amount of the benefit, therefore, is variable depending on the future earnings of the fund, length of service of the employee, etc. The second category involves a definite benefit which is usually, though not necessarily, related to the employee's earnings. Definite benefits of necessity make payments into the fund variable for the same reasons that make benefits variable under the money-purchase scheme. Most industrial pension plans are of the definite-benefit type.

Past Service. Pension plans are almost invariably retroactive in the sense that benefits are based on the total service of the employee, not just his service after adoption of the plan. This means, of course, that a substantial unpaid obligation for these past service benefits comes into being at the moment the plan becomes effective. Furthermore, the problem of past service benefits may be a recurring one for any time the benefits or coverage of a pension plan are increased a new obligation resulting from past service arises. Paying for past service benefits is an area of major difference among pension plans, and accounting for them is quite frequently most unsatisfactory.

Funding. A number of different methods are in current use for providing for the costs of pension plans. These will be considered presently, but before doing so it is necessary to understand that the precise amount of the obligation for pension benefits can never be known in advance. Some assumption must be made about both future market values and earnings rates of pension-fund investments. Changes in either of these will, of course, affect the amount in the fund at any time. A decrease in the number of employees or a change in the rate of turnover of employees will upset the calculations of amounts required to meet future benefit payments. These matters can be and are taken into account by actuaries when setting up a plan, but a degree of uncertainty remains about the exact amount of the liability arising from a pension plan.

126

The soundest method of providing for the cost of future pension benefits involves annual payments into a fund which are equal to the cost of current service benefits plus some reduction or amortization of incurred past service benefits. Both of these can be determined actuarially, although selecting the rate of payment of the liability for past service benefits is inevitably somewhat subjective. There is obviously a conflict between the desirability of complete solvency for the fund which would require immediate payment of the full past service liability and the drain on the company's resources which probably requires spreading the annual payments over a period as long as possible while still reasonably safe. In the case of a single employee it is only necessary that past service benefits be paid in before he retires. When many employees are involved, the rate of payment is perforce based on an average of times to retirement and therefore somewhat uncertain. Ten-year and thirty-year periods are the most common rates of payment, although many other rates are in use.[3]

To qualify for favorable treatment under income-tax regulations, a pension plan must, as a minimum, fund all current costs, which are defined as the cost of current service costs plus the assumed interest on the present value or unfunded portion of past service costs. In effect, this means that the cost of past service benefits is not being funded. No doubt because of this minimum requirement of the Treasury Department, many pensions are funded in this way. (Treasury regulations also permit a maximum deduction for tax purposes of 10 per cent per year for costs of past service benefits. This no doubt explains the popularity of the ten-year amortization period referred to in the previous paragraph.)

A less desirable procedure from the point of view of soundness is so-called terminal funding. Under this procedure no funding is done prior to the employee's retirement. At that time, a single payment is made in an amount sufficient, on an

---

[3]Leonard Lorenson, "Pension Costs in Selected Financial Statements," *Journal of Accountancy*, Vol. 113, No. 3 (March 1962), p. 61.

actuarial basis, to meet the future benefit payments to the retired employee.

Finally, some pension plans are operated without any funding at all. They are on a "pay-as-you-go" basis which means that benefits are paid directly to retired employees out of the company's treasury at the time the benefits are due. Obviously, such plans are least desirable from the employee's point of view since they leave him completely dependent for his pension on the company's financial state at that future time when he retires.

The Accounting Problems

The basic accounting problem is clear. Should corporate financial reports show the full extent of the highly probable future liability for pension benefits whether corporation management has funded the liability or not? Should the best possible estimate of cost—past, present and future—be included in the measurements of annual income? Or to put the question more bluntly, should accountants follow a procedure which best serves the needs of those who are evaluating corporate status and prospects, even if in doing so they depart from accounting for what management has done?

From the point of view of the pensioner-to-be there seems no disputing that a full funding of all benefits (past service and current service to date) is the most satisfactory procedure. Such a fund is the best measure of the present value of a future liability and consequently seems the required basis for accounting for the pension plan.

Companies frequently give two grounds for not fully funding pension plans and therefore, by implication, for not accounting for the full liability. The first of these arguments stresses the absence of any legal obligation to continue the plan, which means that the corporation's legal liability is only for those amounts which have vested in the employees at any time. The second of these arguments is based on the premise that the entire fund will never be claimed at one time. That is, benefits due to one employee can be met from contributions on behalf of an employee not to be pensioned for some time. In a sense this is robbing Peter to pay Paul, although given a more-or-less even distribution of annual retirements, in terms of both numbers of employees and amounts of their pensions, such a policy is not necessarily unsound financially.

The response to the first of these arguments has already been given. The overwhelming social acceptance and approval of pension plans almost surely represent a *de facto* constraint on management's freedom to curtail a pension plan—legalities notwithstanding. That the full amount of the liability will never be claimed at one time can be accepted as a sufficiently sound and prudent basis for financial management. It is not, however, a basis for stating the actual liability of the corporation, and statement of the liability and the related cost is the function of accounting. Incidentally it is interesting to observe the mutual incompatibility of these two arguments. Paying benefits to one person out of contributions in respect to another is obviously based on the assumption of indefinite continuation of the plan. It would not be possible if a plan were discontinued.

Thus, sound accounting for pension plans should show the actuarially determined amount of the present liability under pension plans. That is, all benefits incurred to date including all past service benefits should be shown in financial statements. (Because of the various factors mentioned earler, which can affect these actuarial calculations, they should be revised regularly.) Furthermore, the financial reports should state the amount funded to date. The funds will, of course, be included in the amount of the corporation's resources unless they have been deposited with a trustee or used to purchase future benefits from an insurance company or similar institution.

As far as income determination is concerned, the annual increments in the future liability for pension benefits is clearly an appropriate deduction from realized gross income. Pension plans are obviously a cost of the business. The proper timing of deductions for past service benefits raises something of a problem because in most cases the amount of the cost involved will be greater than can be absorbed by realized gross income in the first year after adoption of the plan. Most accountants argue that pension costs are costs of future years after adoption of the plan and therefore maintain that all costs should be deducted in future periods and conversely none of the costs should be deducted from retained earnings at the time of the adoption of the plan. This is not an unreasonable approach from the point of view of income determination, but it is unreasonable in terms of valuation of resources and claims against them. Once a pension plan is instituted the corporation has a future liability on account of past service. This claim of employees has legal precedence over the claims of stockholders. Consequently, the claim should be shown and should, if necessary, be deducted from the claim of stockholders represented by retained earnings. Ultimately, of course, there will be no difference between this procedure and the procedure of amortizing past service costs over a period of years. At the conclusion of the amortization period, the amount of retained earnings, all else being the same, will be identical in either case. In the one case, an obligation of the corporation is always shown; in the other case it is not.

Current Accounting Practice. The AICPA Accounting Procedure Committee has recommended, in *Bulletin #47*, that pension-plan accounting should include "... costs based on current and future services ... systematically accrued during the expected period of active service of the covered employees, generally on the basis of actuarial calculations." Furthermore, the committee has recommended that "costs based on past services should be charged off over some reasonable period. . . ."[4] In other words, accounting for pension plans should not be governed by the actual funding (or nonfunding) procedures of the corporation. The committee has not, of course, accepted the view stated here that the full liability for past service benefits should be recognized at once.

With typical caution, however, the committee recognized that at the time (1956) its recommendations were somewhat in advance of general practice and so sanctioned *pro tempore*

---

[4]American Institute of Certified Public Accountants, *Accounting Research Bulletin 47* (New York, 1956) para. 5.

a minimum standard of "accruals which equal present worth, actuarially calculated, of pension commitments to employees to the extent that pension rights have vested in the employees."[5] It is an interesting illustration of the extreme deliberation with which accounting principles evolve that according to a recent study, "a significant number of companies" are still meeting the *pro tempore* minimum standard and not accounting for full actuarial costs.[6]

Summary. There seems little doubt that private corporation pension plans are here to stay. There is also no doubt that they represent future claims of very substantial proportions on the resources of our corporations. A proper evaluation of corporate status and affairs cannot be made without full information about pension plans and such information should include the full amount of the present and future liability under the pension plan as well as the amount of this liability which has actually been met by payments into a fund.

III

STOCK OPTIONS

To some, stock options are one of the main sources of strength and growth in the American economy. Henry Ford II, businessman, believes they are in the public interest because they "foster both the most efficient use and the most economical allocation of one of our scarcest and most precious natural resources—management."[7] To others, stock options are discriminatory and immoral devices which strike at the foundations of our society. J. A. Livingston, financial editor, states that, "Executives have become an overprivileged class in a democratic society. Their power to overpay themselves without legal sanction, could, if unchecked, erode the very structure on which

---

[5]*Ibid.*, para. 7.

[6]Lorenson, *loc. cit.*

[7]Henry Ford II, "Stock Options Are in the Public Interest," *Harvard Business Review*, Vol. 39, No. 4 (July-August, 1961), p. 51.

they and their corporations depend for survival.[8] A somewhat more temperate critic, Peter Drucker, suggests that stock options "really provide a businessman's gain without a businessman's risk, or offer extra pay only for doing one's best. These are hardly compatible with the professional role of the executive."[9]

These views are representative of the wide range of opinions about stock options. Discussion of these opinions and others is not relevant to my purpose here although I must observe in passing that my views are much closer to those of Messrs. Livingston and Drucker than to those of Mr. Ford. What is relevant here is that such extreme controversy creates a certain need for complete and detailed accounting for stock options. And if this is not sufficient grounds for absolute exposure to all who are concerned with corporate affairs, the limitation of stock options to a few top managers (who in a practical sense grant them to themselves) certainly is.

Characteristics of Stock Options

Whether it is concluded that stock options are a source of good or of evil, there is no apparent dispute over the fact they accomplish that good or evil through being legalized evasion of high personal-income tax rates. Thus the discussion which follows is confined to the so-called restricted stock option which qualifies for special tax treatment. Without this treatment, stock options would be a most insignificant matter.

The essential characteristics of restricted options are, in brief, the following: the price at which the option may be exercised must be at least 95 per cent of the fair market value of the stock at the time the option is granted. The stock must be held for two years after the option was exercised. In other words, to qualify for special tax treatment, stock may be purchased eighteen months after granting of the option and sold

---

[8]J. A. Livingston, *The American Stockholder* (New York: J. B. Lippincott, 1958), p. 222.

[9]Peter F. Drucker, "Big Business and the National Purpose," *Harvard Business Review*, Vol. 40, No. 2, (March-April, 1962), p. 58.

six months after purchase or two years after the option was received. If these conditions are met, any gain over the option price is tax free to the holder as long as the stock is held—even by his estate after the holder dies. If the stock is sold, the gain is taxed as a capital gain rather than as ordinary income. If the option price is between 85 per cent and 95 per cent of fair market value on the date the option was granted, a somewhat more complicated and less favorable set of rules applies. If the recipient of the option holds more than 10 per cent of the corporation's stock, there are still further qualifications. The "95 per cent option," however, is the most common and is assumed in the discussions which follow. The foregoing describes only the requirements for special tax treatment; it does not necessarily describe actual option plans which may, for example, require that the option not be exercised for a period of three or more years and generally limit the period during which the option is outstanding.

Definition of Cost

Most discussions of accounting for stock options go into the question of whether or not they represent compensation of the executives who receive them. There seems no reason to doubt that they do. In his discussion of stock options Henry Ford II uses such phrases as "to provide incentives for them [managers] to work most effectively and productively," and "reward commensurately with their contribution." These are obvious descriptions of compensation. Whether they are precise substitutes for more conventional compensation is another question. However, does it really make any great difference, in terms of proper accounting, whether stock options are compensation either for past or future service, an investment in executive talent, or little more than a way of recognizing that the optionee is a pleasant fellow? The important accounting function is the measurement of the cost to the corporation of granting the option and this measurement should not be influenced by reasons for incurring the cost. The amount of the cost, on the other hand, is of great importance in evaluating the wisdom

133

or propriety of incurring it. In the days when the ceremonial gold watch was the symbol of corporate eminence, evaluation was not important because cost was insignificant. Stock options may involve millions.

The difficulty with stock options is that their cost must be imputed, and accountants in particular have long been reluctant to have anything to do with imputed costs. In the conventional monetary sense, no cost is incurred because rather than spending money the corporation treasury actually receives money when the employee purchases stock under an option. The cost of options must be imputed in terms of the opportunities the corporation loses by entering into and completing the option arrangement. (This, of course, has no necessary connection with what the corporation gains by the stock option. Mr. Ford and Mr. Drucker, for example, would view this matter quite differently.)

When a corporation sells stock to an executive under an option plan it loses the opportunity to sell the stock to someone else at a higher price. (An executive holding an option is not likely to exercise it if current market price is less than option price. In fact, during the stock market decline of 1957-1958 some corporations canceled options outstanding and reissued them at a price below the new and lower level of market prices. As Erwin Griswold has suggested, this makes options truly a "heads-I-win, tails-you-lose" proposition for executives who hold them.[10]) The cost of the option to the issuing corporation represented by this lost opportunity is the difference between the market price of the stock and the option price when the stock is sold.

Some writers have also included as a part of option cost the tax deductions which would result from equivalent salary payment. Under tax laws, no cost to the corporation is recognized in connection with stock options. Salary payments, of course, are deductible for tax purposes and the corporation's income-

---

[10]Erwin N. Griswold, "Are Stock Options Getting Out of Hand?" *Harvard Business Review*, Vol. 38, No. 6 (November-December, 1960), pp. 52-53.

tax obligation (all else being equal) is reduced (at present rates) by 52 cents for every dollar being paid in salary. Therefore it might be concluded that 52 per cent of the value of the lost opportunity associated with the option is an additional cost of the option.

There are two difficulties with this approach. In the first place, if one is to think in terms of equivalent benefit to the executive, one must think of *after-tax* benefit since the monetary attractiveness of the option is a function of the tax concession involved. Because of different tax treatment, equivalent salary payment would not yield the same *after-tax* income to the executive. Therefore, the alternative salary payment required might be substantially different from the opportunity costs of the option. A recent study[11] suggests that in most cases the salary equivalent which would yield an after-tax break-even with an option benefit to the employee would have to be substantially larger; but somewhat surprisingly, it actually would be lower in a significant number of cases.

The second difficulty with this approach lies in the assumption that a salary payment is the only alternative to a stock option. Some form of deferred compensation (discussed below) might be a suitable alternative. Perhaps the executive would have demanded a higher *after-tax* benefit to compensate for the loss of status resulting from being without options. Perhaps he would have settled for lower after-tax benefit and a thicker Bigelow on the floor. The cost of any of these alternatives net of tax deductions to the corporation will almost surely be different from one another.

In terms of making a decision to grant options or to do something else, the cost of all of the possible alternatives must be considered. If one is attempting to evaluate the wisdom or efficiency of a decision to grant options, the cost of other actions which could have been taken is relevant to the analysis. However, one cannot make an easy generalization about what the

---

[11] D. M. Hall and W. G. Lewellen, "Probing the Record of Stock Options," *Harvard Business Review*, Vol. 40, No. 2 (March-April, 1962).

alternative would have been and one can be quite sure that its cost would not be equal to the opportunity cost of the option. Selection and costing of an alternative to a stock option involves some highly subjective considerations and some important assumptions. And the facts and assumptions will be different for each executive. Consequently, the objectives of accounting seem best served by limiting the definition of the cost of the options to the value of the lost opportunity to sell the stock to someone else.

Determination of Cost

Actually, to implement the concept of cost presented above requires determination of the point at which the corporation loses the opportunity to sell the stock to someone other than the holder of the option. The market value, which is the basis for measuring the opportunity cost, is determined at that date prior to which the opportunity has not been lost and after which the opportunity no longer exists. In most discussions, three different dates are considered.

1. The date the executive is granted the option.
2. The date the executive can exercise the option under the agreement and under relevant tax law.
3. The date the executive actually exercises the option.[12]

Grant Date

The current official position of the AICPA Committee on Accounting Procedure, as indicated in *Bulletin* #43, Chapter

---

[12]A fourth date, when stock acquired under option is sold, is sometimes considered, but it seems completely irrelevant since after purchase of the stock the position of the executive holding the stock is essentially that of an ordinary stockholder: decisions to hold or to sell are purely personal investment decisions and are in no way different from those made about stock acquired with cash received as a bonus, for example. The peculiar link with the corporation which characterizes a stock option is broken as soon as the stock is paid for and subsequent changes in the value of the investment are entirely the result of the executive's financial shrewdness or luck, as the case may be. In fact, the after-tax benefit of a stock option will always be partly a result of the executive's investment decision rather than entirely accruing from corporate munificence, because he cannot realize the tax benefit involved unless he holds the stock for at least six months after purchase.

13, is that cost of stock options to the issuing corporation is the difference between option price and fair market value on the date the option is granted. The committee's reasoning is indicated in the following excerpt from the bulletin:

. . . The date on which an option is granted to a specific individual would be the appropriate point at which to evaluate the cost to the employer, since it was the value at that date which the employer may be presumed to have had in mind. In most of the cases under discussion, moreover, the only important contingency involved is the continuance of the grantee in the employment of the corporation, a matter very largely within the control of the grantee and usually the main objective of the grantor. Under such circumstances it may be assumed that if the stock option were granted as part of an employment contract, both parties had in mind a valuation of the option at the date of the contract; and accordingly, value at that date should be used as the amount to be accounted for as compensation.

This measure of cost does not fit the criteria given earlier, for the corporation in granting the option has not given up the opportunity to sell the stock to someone else. It has agreed that it will give up the opportunity at some future date if certain conditions—principally continued employment—are met, but this is not the same as actually giving up the opportunity and thereby incurring a cost. The practice of canceling options in a period of declining market prices is a good indication that there is nothing very final about the date of granting an option. Basing cost on the date of granting the option has the virtue of leaving no loose ends to be tidied up at some future time. However, untidy though it may be, it is true that the basic criterion for establishing the value which the corporation gives up—which is the cost of granting the option—is not known at the time the option is granted.

Date Exercised

The dates on which the option can be exercised and on which it is exercised presumably will be the same in a great many cases. If the option holder is short of funds to purchase the stock, or if he anticipates a decline in the market price before the date the option expires, he may defer exercising the option. He gains nothing by delaying if he has the money and if he expects a rising or stable market price. Indeed, since he must hold the stock for six months to get special tax treatment, it is advantageous to buy immediately in order to be in a position of freedom of action with tax benefit intact as soon as possible.

If for the reasons given above the date of exercising the option is later than the date at which it became exercisable, the former is the one which fits the definition of cost given here. The corporation does not irrevocably give up the right to sell the stock to someone else and therefore incurs the cost of lost opportunity until the employee has exercised his option and purchased his stock. On the exercisable date the employee has a complete right to use his option, but the use of that right is contingent upon continued employment. (To obtain special tax treatment, the executive must use the option within three months after ceasing to be an employee of the corporation. In most option plans the corporation requires continued employment as a condition of exercise.)

It is true that holding but not exercising the option involves an essentially personal investment decision on the part of the employee. However, it is a decision not to buy and as such has no effect on the opportunities of the corporation. Only when the decision to buy is made and implemented does the corporation lose the opportunity whose value is its cost of granting the option. The difference between the price at which the stock is sold under the option and the price for which it could have been sold in the open market on the date of sale is the before-tax cost of the option to the corporation.

Annual Deductions

There is some objection to this procedure because it defers accounting for a corporate decision until sometime in the future.[13] This objection has led to various proposals for making

---

[13]For fuller statements of this view see W. R. Ruby, "Accounting for Employee Stock Options," *The Accounting Review*, Vol. XXXVII, No. 1, (January 1962), and Edwin D. Campbell, "Stock Options Should be Valued," *Harvard Business Review*, Vol. 39, No. 4 (July-August, 1961).

an annual deduction for stock-option cost during the period the option is in force. One way of doing this would be to use the market price of the corporation's stock on each accounting date. The difference between it and option price would be "cost for the year." The other approach suggested is to estimate what market price will be on the exercise date and thus estimate cost. This cost would be considered as a deferred expense and would be proportionately deducted from realized gross revenue during each year the option was outstanding. A terminal adjustment would be required to bring the forecast and actual market values together on the exercise date.

Either of these procedures certainly conforms to the traditional accounting procedure of matching expenses with the accounting periods which receive the benefit. Or they do this if someone who can predict stock market behavior three, four, or five years hence can be found. (After the stock-market break of May and June, 1962, one must reflect upon the many easy generalizations about the use of future stock prices in accounting and in business decision making generally which have filled the literature and poured forth from the lecture platforms since the end of World War II. I hope my students do not regularly refer to their old class notes.) In light of the possibility of extreme disparity between estimated or interim market prices and market price when the option is exercised (if it is exercised) a procedure for annual charges seems a generally uncertain refinement. This is particularly so when one considers that full disclosure of the details of options outstanding can and should be included in all corporate reports. (See below.) Evaluation of the efficiency and wisdom of the use of stock options must utilize, among other things, knowledge of the cost of the options to the corporation, and this can be known with tolerable certainty only when the cost is actually incurred.

Market Value

One matter, of limited concern in terms of the large corporations which are the subject of this book, remains to be disposed of. The measure of cost of stock options outlined here assumes the existence of a market value of the corporation's stock. For many smaller corporations, and for some larger ones, there may be no market value as such because the stock is not regularly traded. In such cases the stock must be valued on the date of sale by the accountant or some other qualified and independent person. All the usual problems of valuation will be faced, but they are no more insurmountable in this case than in any other.

Disclosure

Pensions and stock options are not the only devices for compensation which have been developed in recent decades primarily in reference to high personal-income tax rates. In addition to various types of insurance, there are liberal expense accounts and devices for deferring compensation. Under one form of arrangement part of the executive's contracted compensation is not paid to him until after he is sixty-five and retired. Because his post-retirement income will be smaller than his preretirement income, it will be taxed at a lower rate. The postretirement consultant is becoming a fixture of the corporate scene, for executives are given contracts for consulting services to be rendered (and paid for) after retirement. That some of these contracts are transferable to the executive's wife after his death is perhaps an indication of the quantity and quality of service expected.

The actual accounting for these other forms of compensation involves no particular problems, for the sums paid will be included in the corporation's expenses. The problem, or rather the absolute necessity, is that all details of these transactions be fully disclosed to all who have an interest in the corporation. Precise rules to cover all situations are difficult to specify, but as a minimum the full details of all of the compensation of all senior officers of a corporation should be disclosed in its regular reports. Certainly, the details of any out-of-the-ordinary forms of compensation such as stock options, bonuses, and deferred compensation should be publicized. In the case of stock options the number of shares under option, the option price, and the market price of the stock at the date of the report should be disclosed.

It can be argued that it is unfair, in many ways, to the

corporation executive to require that his personal remuneration be made a matter of public knowledge. However, as Louis Brown said in the passage quoted in the beginning of this book, a manager "functions on the basis of a trusteeship" and is "accountable to his working organization, to his customers, and to the public." In matters of compensation, management is, for all practical purposes, dealing with itself. The traditional arm's length, that rather quaint but useful lawyer's concept, is considerably shortened in the case of management compensation. In an area where the *possibility*, which is not to say the *actuality*, of self-serving exists, accounting must be fullest. Disclosure may be unfair, but it is surely a part of trusteeship, of accountability, and of responsibility.

Chapter Eleven

INTANGIBLE RESOURCES

I

Emerson may have been right about the mousetrap in nineteenth-century America, but in our time the race toward business success is less likely to be won by him who can make things than by him who can make people buy things. As partial vindication of Emerson's prescience, however, he who can discover new things which people can be made to want to buy is even more likely to be a winner.

Consider soap. People have been making soap since pre-Roman times. It is an overstatement to say that anyone can make soap on a commercial scale, but to do so requires neither the skill involved in making electronic computers, for example, nor the capital required in making steel. Soap making is relatively simple, yet most of our soap is made and sold by three corporations. Success in the soap business is surely dependent on the ability to make people buy a particular brand of soap. Names like "Ivory," "Palmolive," "Lux" are far more important resources than are soap kettles and inventories of fats and oils.

Consider Scotch Tape. With the first marketing of that product America had not only a new way of fastening things; it had a new word. My children and their friends regularly use the verb "to scotch tape" and just as regularly use the adjective "scotch taped." The Minnesota Mining and Manufacturing Company was one among a number of moderate-size companies making sandpaper and other abrasives at the time it introduced Scotch Tape. The success of this new product and continued development of new products have transformed it into a major industrial organization. Success started with finding a new product people would want to buy.

Twenty-five years ago public relations men were largely concerned with the field of entertainment. Today they are often as deeply involved in many corporate decisions as are the production, marketing, and financial experts. Creation and maintenance of a good "corporate image" is now a major concern of corporations and business decisions are carefully studied for their possible effect on the corporate image.

In our consumption-oriented society, competitive position and growth, even survival, seem to be as much dependent upon the corporation's ability to induce consumption by promoting existing products and by discovering new ones as on the traditional ability to produce a good product at a competitive price. The resources required to find new products and to induce consumption are at least as important as the resources required for production. Yet because these resources are generally intangible, in the sense that they do not have the obvious substance of factories, lathes, calculating machines, cash, etc., they are given far less attention by accountants and most others interested in the corporation than are financial resources and resources required for production. Given the importance of the large corporation in our society, the attendant needs of investors, employees, customers, suppliers, and the public generally for reliable information about the corporation are great indeed. Consequently, the lack of such information about important corporate resources and important corporate activities is particularly grievous.

II

There are two broad classifications of intangible resources: those related to some sort of contractual arrangement and those usually labeled "good will." Contractual intangibles are such things as patents, licenses, copyrights, leases, etc. These generally represent a legal right to possess something or to do something —a legal monopoly in the case of patents and copyrights, the use of processes or facilities in the case of licenses or leases. The legal right is normally held for a specified and limited time.

Good will is a name given to earning power whose source cannot be specifically identified. It may result from successful research and development, from a trade name or a good corporate image, from an efficient distribution system or manufacturing know-how. Such a listing could be extended almost indefinitely. The important thing is that the earning power of most successful corporations cannot be attributed entirely to the financial resources, to the buildings and equipment and inventories it owns or controls. This "extra something" is what is called good will.

Actually, the difference between good will and contractual intangibles is not so great as is implied by the distinction made here. The possession of some legal right has economic values only if the right is a source of potential earning power. A patent on a machine for making horseshoes is certainly an exclusive legal right, but it is hardly a significant business resource in 1962. A patent will undoubtedly increase the value to its owner of an otherwise successful product, but it will not make the product successful. Thus the value of contractual intangibles, when they have any value at all, is in large measure related to good will.

The value and the economic life of intangibles are inextricably related. Where there is value there is life. Where there is life there is value. In the case of intangibles, both value and economic life are highly uncertain matters. A well-known brand name can disappear virtually overnight. Several generations of good will ("Ask the Man Who Owns One") did not save the Packard automobile. A product which gives every promise of being a great success may finally be a complete failure, in which case the research which went into it and the patent which protects it from competition are basically without value. The tremendous development and promotion of the Edsel earned no profits. On the other hand, highly successful products such as

"Toni" home permanent waves and "Lestoil" liquid cleaner rocketed the value of small and previously obscure companies. Economic life and value of intangible resources are among the most uncertain of all business facts.

Even where a patent is involved, life and value are uncertain. A patent gives the holder a legal monopoly over a product or process for seventeen years. However, the ultimate value of the patent depends on the marketability of the patented process or product. The market may disappear well before the end of the seventeen years, or may extend well beyond that time. (In the latter case, value to the patent holder would surely decline after seventeen years because the market would have to be shared with competitors.)

Intangible resources may be purchased by a corporation from another owner or they may be developed by the corporation itself. Patents and trade-marks are sometimes purchased directly. Good will most frequently changes hands as a result of the purchase of one company by another. In such cases, the price paid for the purchased company exceeds the value of its net tangible resources and this excess presumably represents the value of its good will. Good will which has been developed by a corporation presumably results from the expenditure of resources on advertising and promotion, research and development, administrative talent, etc. Ultimately, of course, the value of an intangible resource (or any other kind of resource) is quite independent of how it came into the possession of its owner. The value, at any time subsequent to its acquisition, of a machine made by a company for its own use is not, for that reason, different from the value of a similar machine purchased from another. And in this sense, a brand name, for example, is no different from a machine. This distinction between purchased intangibles and "home-grown" intangibles is made here only because it is a distinction generally made in contemporary accounting practice. The distinction is not relevant to the later discussion of alternatives to this practice.

145

III
CONTEMPORARY ACCOUNTING PROCEDURES

Characteristically, extreme caution has been the general response of accounting to the uncertainty which surrounds the existence and the value of intangible resources. In no other area of accounting is the convention of conservatism so much relied upon. Avoiding the risk of overvaluation is sought through deliberate undervaluation. In this, as in other areas, accounting is extremely permissive for one can choose from among recognized procedures which will give virtually opposite results. A recent study[1] suggests that the extreme permissiveness characterizing accounting for intangible resources can, in the aggregate, affect corporate net income in the United States by as much as $5 billion annually, depending upon accounting methods selected.

Resource Valuation

Historical acquisition cost is the usual basis for the valuation of intangibles—that is, the price paid for the intangible provides the quantitative basis for accounting. In the case of good will, the purchase transaction also provides the basis for recognition of the resource—which means that good will is not recognized in the accounts and statements of a corporation unless it has been purchased. For example, when a corporation purchases a successful brand name from a smaller competitor there is a conventional sale and purchase transaction and the price agreed upon provides a historical cost upon which to base accounting for a trade-mark. But what of the brand name developed by a corporation through an advertising and promotion campaign carried on over several years? In such cases, the costs of the campaign are included among operating expenses as they are incurred and there is no historical cost in the conventional sense. If an intangible resource is purchased outside the corporation, it is recognized and valued in the accounts. If the same intangible

---

[1]Stephen H. Wales, "Intangible Expenses and Amortizing Intangible Assets," *Accounting Review*, Vol. XXXVII, No. 1 (Jan. 1962).

resource is developed within the corporation, it is neither recognized nor valued in the accounts.

An exception to the foregoing is usually found in the case of contractual intangibles. When a patent, for example, is taken out on a product or process developed by the corporation itself, the legal, clerical, and other costs associated with obtaining the patent are typically taken as the value of the patent which is included among the company's resources. Nevertheless, this accounting valuation of such a patent is almost surely different from the valuation of the same patent purchased from an outsider, for the price paid in the latter case would surely be based on expected future earnings.

Income Determination

In theory, operating costs associated with intangible resources are taken into net income in accordance with the rules for matching income and expense. Costs are deducted from gross income realized as a result of the expenditure. In practice, this rule is not always followed. The treatment of intangibles not purchased described above is an obvious exception. In that case, the costs associated with the intangible are, in effect, deducted *before* the intangible actually comes into being. For example, the development of a new product may involve several years of work in the corporation's laboratory before it can be marketed. However, the development costs associated with the product have been deducted from gross income before any income is realized from the product.

In the case of intangibles purchased from others or of costs associated with contractual intangibles developed by the corporation itself, a variety of procedures is available and all are used. The costs are sometimes deducted from gross income upon acquisition. That is, acquisition costs are written off immediately. In other cases, the costs are deducted according to some predetermined schedule. For example, amortization over seventeen years is common in the case of patents, no doubt because of the seventeen-year life of the patent. In other cases where there is no legal life to rely upon, an arbitrary period of ten years or twenty years or some other time is used. Finally, in some cases intangibles, especially good will, are never written off. This is often the case with so-called "Good Will Arising from Consolidation." Amortization of good will is not permitted in the determination of taxable income, a fact which may bring about this accounting treatment.

In summary, then, it can be said that accounting for intangible resources is quite thoroughly confused. If the intangible is purchased from another, it will be accounted for in one way or another. If it has been developed by the corporation itself it may not, in effect, be accounted for at all. Operating costs associated with intangibles may be deducted from income before the intangible actually exists, at the time it is acquired, after it is acquired, or never. Truly a procedure for every taste!

IV
THE RATIONALE OF ACCOUNTING PROCEDURES

An explanation of this profusion of accounting procedures must begin with another acknowledgment of the uncertainty which characterizes most intangibles. For example, few people, including most accountants, would deny that good will does exist, that most corporations have value not reasonably attributable to tangible resources. Yet unless it has been purchased and paid for, the accountant is left without any conventional proof of its existence or of its value. One can *say* that ABC Corporation has good will, but one cannot be sure. There is no piece of paper—no bill of sale or voucher—to support the assertion. In such circumstances, the conservative thing to do is to ignore the matter entirely. (It can be argued that even purchase and sale do little to establish the value of good will. They do prove that someone has been willing to pay good money for something other than tangible resources, but while the amount of money may establish historical cost for accounting purposes the uncertainty surrounding good will has not really been eliminated. Its value is a chancey thing and the purchaser may be just as wrong as the seller might have been.) There is no doubt that valuation of good will developed by a corporation involves uncertainty. The fact that the good will was not purchased, however much comfort may be taken from the independent confirmation of value implicit in purchase or sale, does not seem sufficient grounds for ignoring it.

The same considerations are relevant to handling intangibles in income determination. There is no doubt that the probable economic life of an intangible resource cannot be estimated with any great certainty. The "safe," the conservative thing to do in such a case is to deduct all costs immediately. Since we do not know over what period they should be deducted, it is more conservative to get them all deducted before the good will becomes valueless and we find ourselves reporting it as if it still had value. In a great many cases, good will probably increases in value as time goes on, which means that accounting involving immediate or short-term writeoffs is most unrealistic. As Joel Dean has put it, "As markets are established and profits come in, the good will is written off the books. Thus paper good will may be written off as the real good will builds up."[2]

Accounting for intangibles involves two risks. One is the risk of reporting a resource which does not exist. The other is the risk of not reporting a resource which does exist. The associated risks are those of not recording costs which have been incurred or of recording costs which have not been incurred. In the name of conservatism accountants have almost always tried to achieve a complete hedge against the risks of reporting nonexistent resources and of not recording incurred costs. In so doing they have almost surely been extremely misleading about the real value of our corporations.

Discrimination

Accounting procedures for intangible resources and related tax regulations may discriminate significantly in favor of a certain type of corporation. The problem here concerns growth

---

[2]Joel Dean, *Managerial Economics* (Englewood Cliffs, N. J.: Prentice-Hall, 1951), p. 15.

and its relationship with net income. For purposes of illustration, assume that one corporation maintains its competitive position largely through promotion and that another does so largely through production. If both corporations are striving to grow as well as to maintain competitive position, the promotion corporation has a decided accounting and tax advantage. It can make expenditures on promotion aimed entirely at fostering growth and deduct these expenditures from *current* gross income both for accounting purposes and for tax purposes. It does not have to worry about distributing the money required to maintain competitive position and foster growth to the tax collector, the stockholder, the customer, or the worker. The production corporation is in a quite different position. Competitive position and growth may depend upon the purchase of more and better —and more expensive—machinery, but it must compute its net income on the basis of the costs of machinery acquired years before. The tax collector and the worker, the stockholder and the customer all make demands on the profit this company needs for the maintenance of competitive position and growth. Small wonder that most of the outcries against contemporary accounting practice come from the heavy manufacturing companies such as steel.[3]

Corporations relying largely upon advertising and promotion and research and development are able to state their net income more or less in accordance with a competitive position concept of net income. That is, many of the costs they are permitted to deduct from realized gross income are costs incurred in maintaining the corporation's competitive position in the future and thus their net income is, in part, the residue of realized gross income after deduction of the costs of maintaining competitive position. Corporations whose position depends largely on their productive resources are generally stuck with the historical-

---

[3]Both production corporations and distribution corporations are equally able to charge off research and development expenditures, and to the extent that these play an important part in maintaining the position of either type of company no discrimination is involved.

See, for example, *Accounting and Reporting Problems of the Accounting Profession* (Chicago: Arthur Anderson and Co., 1960), section 12.

cost concept of income. Their net income is the residue of realized gross income after deduction of some arbitrary portion of historical monetary costs. These historical monetary costs only infrequently bear any relationship to the costs of maintaining current competitive position and thus these corporations are in a considerably less favorable position, vis-à-vis promotion corporations, simply because of accounting.

V

Broadly speaking, there are three possible approaches to improving contemporary accounting for intangible resources. These will be discussed below, but none can be recommended without considerable qualification. Much more research into accounting for intangibles is needed, and especially is there needed a willingness to experiment with new approaches. The following procedures are suggested as bases for such experimentation and research.

One approach to intangibles is to proceed with extreme conservatism and, in effect, do no real accounting at all. All current expenditures for research, promotion, etc.—indeed all expenditures except those for inventory and fixed-asset acquisition—would be written off when the expenditures were made. The direct purchase of intangibles from another would also be immediately written off. No intangible resources would be shown on corporate balance sheets. All outlays associated with intangible resources would be written off as made regardless of when benefit from expenditures is expected.

About the only advantage this procedure has (but it is an important advantage) is to insure comparability among company statements. It would avoid entirely the uncertainty which inevitably surrounds contemporary accounting procedures. One would at least be sure of what he is *not* reading in corporate reports. Beyond this, the procedure is rather like that of eliminating sin by legalizing it. If it were adopted it would mean that extremely important resources would not be recognized, and any reasonable matching of revenue and expenses would be out of the question. It can be considered an improvement over present uncertain procedures but not a substitute for positive and meaningful accounting for intangibles.

A second approach is to attempt direct evaluations of intangibles based on the costs of acquiring them. In the case of purchased intangibles—good will, patents, licenses, etc.—this is the procedure usually followed in contemporary practice. Accounting for "home-grown" intangibles would involve a capitalization of at least that portion of current expenditures which can be reasonably related to future benefit. That is, the costs of research on a product which will not be perfected for a number of years should not, it is suggested, be deducted from current gross income. Rather these costs should be carried forward to those future periods when income from the product will be realized. At that time, the costs would be deducted in accordance with the expected life of the product. The costs of advertising designed to create markets, perpetuate brand names, and the like would be treated in much the same way.

The foregoing proposal has a great deal of merit primarily because it would achieve a far better matching of revenue and expense. Costs would be deducted from income during the time period when the resources were actually producing income.

A principal difficulty with this approach is the necessity of isolating several different elements implicit in aggregate current expenditures. Some of these are for the creation of future income-producing resources. Other parts of current expenditure are simply for the maintenance of existing intangibles. Intangible resources must be maintained just as machinery must. A brand name must be constantly promoted if it is to continue to attract. Patents often require the protection of further patents on substitutes. The corporate image can become tarnished quite quickly in the absence of constant attention to it. Finally, some expenditures made for future benefit will not be realized. For example, by mid-1961, General Dynamics Corporation had recognized that some $425 million spent in previous years on the development of its Convair 880 and 600 aircraft was, in fact, a total loss.[4]

Furthermore, this procedure does not help particularly during the period in which the intangibles are being used to produce income. It is usually suggested that research and development expenditure, for example, be deducted from income over the estimated life of the product, but what is the life of a new product? How long will a brand name continue to produce income? Does its power to produce income decline gradually or does it expire suddenly and unexpectedly? Any scheme of amortization requires a reasonable estimate of life and, if resource values on balance sheets are to have meaning, a reasonable prediction of decline in value. It seems unlikely that either of these requirements can be met in the case of intangible resources.

One very important thing this procedure would accomplish would be to eliminate in some measure the unwarranted distinction made between intangibles developed by the corporation and those purchased from others. In both cases the existence of the intangibles would be recognized and costs would be deducted while income was being realized from the intangible, albeit imperfectly.

The third possible approach to accounting for intangibles is to work with present values.

There is, after all, no area of accounting where the complete irrelevance of historical cost is more obvious. Intangible resources—especially good will—are almost by definition the present value of future earnings from generally indeterminate sources. The cost of obtaining a patent, of developing a new product, of a campaign to improve the corporate image has very little to do with the value of the patented product, the new product, or the corporate image. Yet because the exact sources of this earning power are not always known, it is not possible to measure their present value. Nor can we resort here to replacement value as a substitute for present value as may on occasion be done with fixed assets, for example. Replacement value in-

---

[4]Richard Austin Smith, "How a Great Corporation Got Out of Control," *Fortune*, Vol. LXV, Nos. 1, 2 (January and February, 1962).

volves identification of the resource to be replaced and one does not always know what the particular intangible is.

The present value of intangible resources can be determined by deduction from the aggregate present value of the corporation. If the present value of financial resources, of inventories, of fixed assets, and of other known resources is deducted from the present value of the whole corporation, the difference should equal the value of the intangible resources of the corporation. The problem, of course, is to achieve a satisfactory method of measuring the present value of the corporation. The market price of the corporation's stock is one possible approach. Another is simply an estimate by the corporation's management.

Over the long run, the market price of a corporation's stock should represent the present worth of the corporation's estimated future earnings, assuming acceptance of the market's appraisal of risk. In the short run, of course, the market is subject to a variety of essentially extraneous factors (Eisenhower's heart attack, Sputnik, etc.). Consequently, a considerable amount of judgment is involved in selecting a market price, and it would undoubtedly be necessary to utilize average prices over some reasonable period of time.

There may also be a certain amount of circular reasoning involved in basing the present value of corporations on the market price of their stock. Investors' decisions to buy or sell securities are largely based on two sources of information—information about expected behavior of the economy as a whole and information about the present status and expected future progress of the corporation in question. This latter source of information is precisely what we are considering here. To the extent that intangible resources are not recognized or are grossly misvalued in corporate reports and statements, the investor must, of course, guess about their worth. Since the guess will not in most cases be an informed guess, it is of doubtful validity as a basis for valuing intangibles.

Management estimates of the value of the corporation are, of course, subject to abuse. The open invitation to appear as one would like to be rather than as one is, is apparent. The value of intangibles is, more than the value of other resources, the result of management effort, and the desire to show this effort as effective would no doubt be strong. Furthermore, the problem of relative optimism or pessimism may unintentionally—even unwittingly—be involved. With a Republican in the White House valuation might tend to be optimistic and relatively high—at least when made by Republican managers. The gloom that a Democratic president seems to cast over most executive dining rooms would surely find its way into valuations.

On the other hand, management has available more and better information than anyone else. Management decisions about advertising and promotion programs, research and development activities, decisions to purchase a patent or a brand name must involve some contemplation of the present value of the corporation and the effect of the decision thereon. (Such contemplation may be most informal and rough, but constant improvements in ability to collect and process data and in the art of using these data result in increasingly sophisticated contemplations.) The essential fact is that management, because of the information it has, is in the best position to estimate the present worth and thereby the value of intangible resources of the corporation. Furthermore, it would be an important function of the public accountant to test the reasonableness of management estimates, utilizing his knowledge of the particular corporation, his ability to compare estimates with those made by other clients, and a knowledge of business conditions generally. The characteristic caution of most accountants should act as an antidote to either excessive optimism or excessive pessimism.

If the value of intangible resources is determined as suggested above, the procedure to be used in income determination follows quite obviously. The change in the present worth of the intangibles from one period to the next, plus or minus current expenditures on advertising, research, contributions and all the other things which enter into the creation of intangibles, would be the income or expense associated with the intangibles. Such a procedure would eliminate the problem of separating out of current expenditures those which are solely for maintenance of existing intangibles rather than for the creation of new ones. In some instances, there would be a net increase in the value of intangibles and therefore income (in the conventional sense) rather than expense. This would create a need to recognize the difference between increases in capital and distributable income. The capital required to maintain the present competitive position of the corporation is just as real in the case of intangibles as it is in the case of cash, receivables, inventory, and plant. Without their brand names, their flow of new products, their image, few of our large corporations would occupy their present competitive position. Increases in such capital arising from increases in present worth of resources of the corporation need not be confused with distributable income.

VI

Reluctantly, one must conclude this discussion on a somewhat tentative note. This is one of those situations where one can be far more forceful about crying with alarm than about suggesting how to put out the fire. It seems beyond dispute that intangible resources represent one of the major problem areas of accounting for the modern large corporation. Even though untried, the procedure just described is conceptually sound. There is no denying that it will, in a way, involve the intrusion into accounting of more subjectivity than has heretofore been tolerated. Attempts at implementation may indicate unsolvable problems, but subjectivity should not be one of them. It is, after all, a subjective conclusion that deliberate, albeit certain, undervaluation is preferable to an honest and intelligent estimate of real value.

The present procedure for accounting for intangibles represents typically a conservative reaction to uncertainty. In effect, it is based on the proposition that if one is not sure what value, if any, a particular resource will have and if one is not sure how long it will continue to have value if it does have any, the safe, conservative thing is to assume it has no value. But there are other possible reactions to uncertainty. Is it better to be virtually certain of being wrong, or is it better to have a reasonable certainty of being right? Is it preferable to rely upon a piece of paper which is evidence of something which happened in the past, or is it preferable to rely upon the experience, intelligence, and integrity of accountants and managers in making estimates about the present and the future? In light of the vital social role of the corporation, every scrap of information about it that can be stated with a *reasonable* degree of reliability should be made available. Because our economy is so much based on consumption we can no longer afford to be ignorant of the resources required to induce consumption. The art of persuasion is no longer very gentle; the hard sell is ours to live with. Neither is it inexpensive, for vast amounts of capital are required to maintain our levels of consumption. The extent of this commitment of resources must be known even if only with a limited degree of certainty.

Chapter Twelve

RESPONSIBILITY FOR ACCOUNTING:. A SUMMING UP

I

The twentieth-century capitalist revolution has brought the large corporation to the very center of our society. There is no doubt that these corporations and their managers are the repository of enormous economic and social power. That this has come about quite without design or plan and that much of the power is unused—perhaps even unrecognized—by those who hold it is beside the point. It is there and it must be responsible. A key requirement in maintaining the responsibility of the holders of power is to put information about the uses of that power into the hands of those to whom the responsibility is owed. It is in terms of this requirement that the foregoing descriptions and discussions of contemporary accounting for the status and progress of large corporations have been made. It is not suggested that financial information—the particular province of accounting—is the sum total of information required. However, it is true that a very great deal of what corporations do or do not do is ultimately expressed in financial terms. Financial information, broadly defined, has a critical role in the evaluation of corporate status and progress.

The coverage in the foregoing pages of controversial areas of contemporary accounting has by no means been exhaustive, but those areas discussed are generally illustrative and are of broadest importance. The conceptual and procedural details have changed from chapter to chapter, but hopefully the reader will have observed a number of fundamental problems underlying every one of the specific issues.

In the first and most important place, there is the need for accounting to re-examine from time to time its basic role in our society and the way it is carrying out that role. Much of accounting's development seems mostly to have been a steady tinkering with nuts and bolts rather than a complete overhaul of the basic machinery. In the words of Leonard Spacek, a most persistent and articulate advocate of change and improvement in accounting:

Instead of standard of measurement, attention is focused on techniques. Most documents are overburdened with procedural comment on how to handle certain transactions, but little is said about the effect sought and still more important—why.[1]

It is always important for any individual or organization to ask itself "why" and never more so than for accounting in these days of rapid and extreme change in the role in society of the corporations being accounted for.

In the second place, there is an obvious need for accounting to be able to change its procedures in accordance with the results of such basic re-examinations as those suggested above and in the face of changes in particular business conditions or techniques.

A third problem, closely related to the second, is the necessity to achieve uniformity and to ensure disclosure of all relevant data. The need to develop new procedures has as a corollary the necessity for discarding old ones. Failure to do so is an important cause of lack of uniformity.

Finally, the inevitability of uncertainty has been a factor in all the problems discussed in this book. Living with uncertainty is largely a matter of understanding and attitudes rather than of organizations and machinery, and discussion of this matter is

---

[1] Leonard Spacek, "The Need for an Accounting Court," *The Accounting Review*, Vol. XXXII, No. 3 (July 1958), p. 369.

deferred until later in this chapter. The first three of these problems—the need to re-examine the basic role of accounting, the need to adopt new conventions and procedures as required, and the requirement for a reasonable degree of uniformity and a necessary degree of disclosure—are all related in the sense that they exist because of the way the accounting profession is organized and functions.

The objectives and procedures proposed in this book seem more in accord with the nature and role of the modern corporation than those implicit in current accounting practice. Unfortunately, there seems to be no sure way in which these propositions (or anyone else's) can be considered, modified, accepted, or rejected by accountants. As Mr. Spacek has said, "Today there is no place where agreement on basic premises can be argued."

The failure to resolve the controversy over price-level adjustments, after more than fifteen years of fairly steady inflation, is an obvious outcome of an inability to re-examine the basic role of accounting and change procedures accordingly. The confused floundering which has been accounting's response to the rapid growth of stock options or leasing is a clear manifestation of inability to resolve, even over ten years, an accounting problem created by a new business technique.

As suggested before, accounting is largely subjective. Conventions and procedures generally cannot be labeled right or wrong. But the relative can be substituted for the absolute: the absence of a right procedure does not preclude the existence of a best procedure. Selection of a best procedure requires some sort of functioning selection machinery, just as uniform use of a best procedure requires machinery for enforcement. As the brief description of the accounting profession which follows will show, there is no such machinery. The development and regulation of accounting theory and practice is basically the result of *ad hoc* expedients, largely dictated by the very corporations whose affairs are being accounted for.

II

To define the accounting profession is a virtually impossible task. The high-school lad who spends his Saturdays keeping the books for the corner grocer may call himself an accountant, as may hundreds of thousands of other people in and out of industry and government who are involved in one way or another with financial record keeping. At a more significant level—that level involving the analysis, interpretation, and reporting of financial data and the development of principles and procedures for so doing—it is possible to distinguish four main groups of accountants.

The first and largest of these are the employees of business, nonprofit organizations, and government. The Financial Executives Institute, The National Association of Accountants, The Institute of Internal Auditors, and several associations of government accountants are among the more important of the professional societies representing this large and heterogeneous group of accountants. These people are for the most part only marginally involved in that area of accounting being discussed here; their primary concern is with accounting data used in internal operating management. However, the senior accounting officers of a corporation play a key role in deciding the extent and the conceptual bases of the corporation's accounting to its several constituencies.

A second, and much smaller group, are the teachers of accounting. Since few of these men are or ever have been practitioners, and since their qualifications are more likely to be academic than professional, it is possibly inappropriate to list them as accountants. However, some of these men have had a profound influence upon the practice of accounting through their research and publication as well as through their teaching. The American Accounting Association, the professional organization of teachers of accounting, has through its meetings and publications made important contributions to the structure and practice of accounting.

A third part of the accounting profession consists of members of a wide range of government agencies. Some of these agencies have power, granted by the legislation which created them, to prescribe accounting regulations in one way or another. The Securities and Exchange Commission has wide powers over accounting procedures and standards for corporations whose securities are publicly traded. The Interstate Commerce Commission, representative of a group of agencies, has complete control over the accounting of the carriers under its jurisdiction. Other government agencies do not have statutory power to specify accounting principles and practices but have great influence through their other powers. The Internal Revenue Service is, of course, foremost among these and a number of instances in which its regulations concerning taxable income have influenced accounting generally were described in preceding chapters.

Most important in terms of the matters being discussed here are the public accountants, some of whom are designated as Certified Public Accountants, many of whom are not. The Certified Public Accountants, particularly those members of the eight large firms which dominate the profession,[2] are the persons most directly concerned with the accounting for our large corporations. These are the men who certify the statements of most of these corporations. The *Accounting Research and Terminology Bulletins* of their American Institute of Certified Public Accountants collectively represent the closest thing to an authoritative statement of contemporary accounting principles and procedures.

For the most part no laws grant Certified Public Accountants a pre-eminence or authority over accounting. The regulations of the Securities and Exchange Commission and the several stock exchanges, as well as some state laws and some corporation charters, require statements of corporations to be examined and certified by an "independent" public accountant. This requirement does give the public accountant, and especially the CPA's

---

[2]T. A. Wise, "The Auditors are Comming," *Fortune*, November, 1960 and December, 1960. These two articles contain an excellent description of the organization and functioning of public accountants. The second article also briefly discusses some of the problems which are the concern of this book.

as generally acknowledged leaders of public accounting, a certain status and an implied responsibility for developing and maintaining accounting principles and procedures. It is only an implied responsibility, however, for the CPA has no authority, statutory or implied, over any of the other groups which make up the accounting profession. Even within the American Institute of CPA's "general acceptance" is the only real basis for authority. The membership has the authority to vote rules of practice, but has done so in only six relatively noncontroversial instances since 1932.[3] General acceptance, as illustrated by many procedures cited earlier, tends to mean "anything goes."

Authority of Management

Given the profusion and confusion of "professionals" just described it is not surprising that the real authority over accounting for corporations rests primarily with those who have the ultimate power—the managements of the corporations whose status and progress are being accounted for. Virtually all writings concerned with corporate financial reporting begin with the disclaimer that the reports are managements' reports. The Introduction to the *Accounting Reseach and Terminology Bulletins* puts it this way:

> Underlying all committee opinions is the fact that the accounts of a company are primarily the responsibility of management. The responsibility of the auditor [i.e. public accountant] is to express his opinion concerning the financial statements and to state clearly such explanations, amplifications, disagreement or disapproval as he deems appropriate.

The nub of the whole problem of independent control of accounting by accountants is implicit in the last sentence of this statement. As Leonard Spacek has written with considerable candor, the accountant "can swallow his convictions or he can qualify his opinion, or he can resign. Usually the latter two courses are one and the same."[4] Public accountants are hired

---

[3]American Institute of Certified Public Accountants, *Accounting Research and Terminology Bulletins* (New York, 1961), chap. 1.
[4]Spacek, *loc. cit.*, p. 371.

and paid by the corporations whose records they are to examine and report upon. It is true that many corporate charters require election by stockholders, but in practice they are nominated by management and election is a matter of routine. The fact that public accountants are dependent upon managements for their livelihood is not in itself destructive of independent control over accounting standards. But the lack of any specific authority of their own combined with the lack of any external standards upon which they can rely does place the public accountant in a most ambiguous position vis-à-vis his clients.

The Securities and Exchange Commission has accounting regulations in force (Regulation S-X and amendments compose the basic statement) but for the most part these are simply a restatement of generally accepted accounting procedures and as such reflect all of the ambiguities, permissivenesses, and uncertainties of these procedures. The commission clearly has the authority to state and require specific accounting procedures, but to date it has not done so.[5] The major stock exchanges also have what may be called minimum regulations, but these, like those of the SEC, are not independently determined. They are the same uncertain standards everyone else has.

Without the sanction of recognized authority, the public accountant is in the position of having to rely almost entirely on his logic and his persuasiveness in supporting his judgment against that of his client. In many instances, the accountant's judgment will be in direct conflict with the apparent best interests of his client and it is therefore not surprising that to a very considerable degree accounting standards have, in fact, been set by the corporations whose affairs are being accounted for. This is not intended to impute wrong motives to corporation managers. The fact is that accounting standards are in large measure set by bargaining between public accountants and corporation managers and in this bargaining the corporation managers hold the balance of power. When their best interests, as

---

[5]For a detailed discussion of the commission's accounting activities see L. H. Rappaport, SEC *Accounting Practice and Procedure* (New York: The Ronald Press Co., 1959), esp. Chap. 2.

they see them, are involved it is not surprising that they use the power to protect them.

III

The basic need is for objective and authoritative accounting standards which will serve the needs of all the constituencies of the corporation. Meeting this need can come only from a combination of greater discipline and authority within the accounting profession and of independence of public accountants from the corporations whose affairs are being accounted for.

Discipline and authority within the accounting profession are necessary to ensure that accounting concepts and procedures change and evolve as business conditions and practices change and evolve, and to ensure the uniformity and the degree of disclosure modern conditions require. Quite simply, there must be some voice which, after adequate investigation of the problem, can say with authority, "This is the way this particular bit of accounting will be done."

Independence of public accountants from corporations could, of course, be achieved by having public accountants appointed and paid by the public, as we do in the case of judges. However, this sort of independence would achieve little without the discipline within the profession discussed above. Furthermore, a well-defined authority within the profession very likely would extend beyond the profession and thus bring about the desired independence. It is, after all, an independent body of accounting doctrine which is needed. Except as a means toward that end, independence of accountants as such is not important.

At present the needed voice of authority exists in the SEC. No new legislation or machinery would be required. The commission could simply replace Regulation S-X with new regulations which in all cases set forth a specific procedure to be followed. In other words, decision of the commission would replace general acceptance by the profession.

Another, and more attractive, possibility is the Accounting

Court suggested by Leonard Spacek.[6] In essence, Mr. Spacek has proposed a panel of independent accounting experts, elected for life by the entire accounting profession. The court would be under the aegis of the AICPA but Mr. Spacek has proposed all sorts of guarantees of its independence. The court would consider all aspects of any particular question of accounting theory or practice (either on its own volition or at the request of others) and hand down a judgment which would, in effect, become the standard for accounting until subsequently revised by the court. The court's opinions would be accounting doctrine. Such a court would certainly provide the necessary authority within the profession. If it became sufficiently prestigious its authority would, no doubt, gradually extend outside the profession. However, a combination of the probable thoroughness and independence of the accounting court with the authority of the SEC seems the most efficacious solution of all. If the opinions of the court were adopted by the SEC as a part of its accounting regulations their authority both within and without the profession would be unquestionable.

Such machinery would go far toward achieving the necessary independent body of accounting doctrine. Debate over accounting concepts, principles, and procedures would be conducted without becoming involved with the question of effects on a particular client's reports and statements. Clients would be entitled to argue for or against a particular proposal before the court, but arguments would have to be on long-run and fundamental questions, not on expediency of the moment. If such a court had been in existence during the past twenty-five years—quite independent and with adequate resources for research—it seems most likely that the sweeping changes which have taken place in the role of corporations would have been accompanied by a searching re-examination of the role of accounting. Many of the diverse and contradictory procedures in use today would surely have been eliminated. It would not have taken ten years to decide how to account for stock options. In short, there would

---

[6]Spacek, *loc. cit.*

have been machinery for a thorough and independent examination of all aspects of a problem followed by an authoritative decision. Whether the particular machinery suggested here is the most suitable is subject to further debate. That there must be some such machinery is not. Changes in our business society are taking place far too rapidly and the number of unresolved accounting problems created by these changes is far too numerous to permit a continuation of an interminable and disorderly evolution away from the standards of an earlier and much different time.

IV

"Accounting seems to flourish in a stable environment, and to languish in an unstable one. Flux, change and disorder are always unsettling." These words of Maurice Moonitz, director of research of the AICPA[7] form a most succinct statement of a fundamental problem of accounting. It seems inevitable that we will continue to be unsettled since flux, change, and disorder are surely the signs of our time. A principal task of accounting is to accept the uncertainty which is their progeny.

Most currently accepted accounting concepts and procedures are based on an expectation of certainty of a sort. Historical cost can be verified; therefore it is certain. Realization can be verified and thus is a certain thing. This dependence upon verification is undoubtedly related to the public accountant's or auditor's traditional function of checking up, of attempting to ascertain that neither theft nor fraud has taken place. Verification obviously is the basis of such activity. This sort of checking up is still an important function, for there is no evidence that the thieves and defrauders among us have become fewer. It is equally important, however, that concepts and procedures appropriate to this policeman function cease to influence that more significant function of accounting which is to provide a basis for communication between corporations and their several constituencies.

---

[7]American Institute of Certified Public Accountants, *The Basic Postulates of Accounting* (Accounting Research Study No. 1) (New York, 1961), p. 9.

Meeting this need requires the best possible statement of the current status and probable future progress of the corporation, which, in a period of flux, change, and disorder, are manifestly not measured by past events no matter how precisely they may be verified.

It has often been said in defense of accounting practice that the reader of a financial statement knows he is reading verifiable facts and not someone's approximation and guesses. The implication is that he is therefore better off. But if these verifiable facts are of little relevance to the judgments and decisions he has to make it is hard to see how he is any better off than the explorer planning an expedition from Little America towards the South Pole with forecasts of weather in Labrador.

Accountants seem to regularly underestimate their own and management's intelligence. Managements regularly base decisions on best estimates of current and probable future values—decisions which in the aggregate involve billions of dollars annually. Those who must evaluate these decisions have a need for access to the same relevant information. Nor does this call for fortunetelling. Replacement value cannot always be verified in the way historical cost can be read from an invoice, but it can be estimated quite closely. Manufacturing know-how cannot be walked about in as can manufacturing facilities, but its existence is generally obvious from the sale of the corporation's products. Investors make valuations of corporations every minute of the day, utilizing far less information than managers and their public accountants have as a matter of course.

Ultimately the issue is certainty versus relevance; the picayune versus the significant. Accounting should be willing to substitute business and economic intelligence and good judgment for routine verification. The accountant must temper the importance of precedent in his activities with an acceptance of and accommodation to change. Only by accepting a broader and more challenging view of its role of furnishing relevant and significant data to the constituencies of the corporation can accounting meet its obligation to the society which is so dominated by the corporation.

V

In concluding both chapter and book, two important implications of much written here should be pointed out.

First, a number of suggestions made involve substantial departures from current accounting practice and some of them will not be easy to implement. Indeed, some of them may have to be modified after trial. However, the fact that there are few precedents for some of these suggestions is not important. In an era when most of society's precedents are disappearing into outer space, it seems important to try any approach which will bring the practice of accounting more closely into accord with the changing social and economic role and objectives of the large corporations for which it is accounting.

Second, many of the suggestions made in this book involve some additional interference in what have traditionally been the exclusive affairs of corporations—some further curtailment of their freedom. The need for this seems clear. The modern large corporation has an important influence on the lives of us all. It has a broad social responsibility which has been accepted by the great majority of corporation managers. A part of responsibility is periodic evaluation by those to whom one is responsible. In this sense, responsibility involves some loss of freedom, but it is quite in accord with our ideas and ideals that responsibility is an important guarantee of freedom.

INDEX

A

Accounting
  as control system, 14
  limited to financial matters, 38-39
  role of, 14-17
  uncertainty in, 167-68
Accounting conventions; *see also
  each convention*
  development of, 31, 40-41
  reluctance to change, 31-32
  subjective origins of, 40
Accounting Court, 166-67
Accounting profession
  described, 161-63
  need for discipline and authority,
    165-66
Accounting Research Bulletins
  Number 43, 136
  Number 47, 130
  Number 48, 120
American Accounting Association,
  34, 161
  Committee on Concepts and
    Standards, 34
American Institute of Certified Public
  Accountants, 24, 26, 29, 34, 86,
  162
  Committee on Accounting
    Research, 31
American Telephone and Telegraph
  Company, 3, 107, 116
Armstrong Cork Company, 36
Avco Corporation, 106, 108

B

Balance sheet defined, 23
  as source of information about
    growth, 23-24
Berle, A. A., Jr., 2, 9
Blough, Carmen, 35
British-American Oil Co., Ltd., 103
Brown, Louis D., 12, 13, 141

C

Capital, bases for valuation of; *see*
  Concepts of value and capital
Capital gains, 59, 72
Changing price levels; *see* Price-level
  adjustments

Charitable contributions, 22, 62
Chrysler Corporation, 34
Comparability in accounting, need
  for, 26-33
Compensation, accounting for, 123-41
Complex business organizations
  forms of, 106-7
  need for information about
    components, 107-10
  need for information about entity,
    110-14
Concepts of value and capital
  competitive-capacity, 60-61
  monetary, 52-53, 72
  present worth, 51-52, 79, 153-56
  productive-capacity, 54-55, 61, 72
  purchasing power, 53-54
Conservatism, convention of, 40, 146,
  149, 156
Consistency, convention of, 41
Consolidated financial statements
  conditions for, 114-17
  defined, 114
  treatment of goodwill arising from,
    117-19
Consumer Price Index; *see* Price-
  level adjustments
Contractual intangible resources,
  143-44, 147
Control, accounting information
  needed for, 15-16
Corporations
  objectives of, 18-23
  responsibilities of, 11-13, 21-22
  role of managers of, 3, 140-41
Cybernetic revolution, 10

D

Dean, Joel, 149
Decline in value of fixed assets
  pattern of decline, 84-85
  recognition of, in accounting, 86-92
  useful life, 83-84
Declining-balance depreciation, 89-90
Deferred compensation of executives,
  disclosure of, 140-41
Deferred income taxes, accounting
  for, 94-98

Depletion, 102
Depreciation, methods of accounting
    for
    constant deductions, 87-88
    decreasing deductions, 89-91
    variable deductions, 88-89
"Direct costing," 73-76
    relationship with replacement cost,
        75-76
Disclosure of accounting methods,
    28-29
Discrimination in accounting for
    intangible resources, 149-51
Drucker, Peter, 132, 134
Du Pont Company, 112

E

Eaton, Marquis, 26, 29
Eisenhower, Dwight D., 9
Electronic data processing
    and corporate growth, 19
    in fixed-asset accounting, 82-83
    in inventory accounting, 71-72

F

FIFO inventory valuation; see In-
    ventory valuation methods
Financial Executives Institute, 161
Fixed-asset accounting, objectives of,
    78, 92-94; see also Depreciation,
    methods of accounting for
Fixed assets, useful life of, 83-84
Ford, Henry II, 131-32, 133, 134
Funds statement
    place in corporate reports, 24
    as source of information about
        growth, 23-24

G

Galbraith, J. K., 19, 20
General Dynamics Corporation, 56,
    152
General Electric Company, 44, 56
General Foods Corporation, 56
General Mills, 56
General Motors Corporation, 3, 56,
    107, 108-9, 112, 116
Gilbert, Lewis D., 11
Goodwill
    arising from consolidation, 117-19,
        148
    defined, 143-44
Griswold, Erwin, 134
Growth as corporate objective, 18-23
Gulf Oil Corporation, 103

H

Hendricksen, E. S., 36
Holding company statements, limited
    value of, 112-14

I

Imperial Tobacco Company of
    Canada, Ltd., 32, 82
Income
    as corporate objective, 2, 18
    determination of, 18
    realized and unrealized, 58, 72, 80,
        104, 156
Income taxation and accounting
    for fixed assets, 78
        deferred taxes, 94-98
    for intangible resources, 148
    for LIFO inventories, 69-70
    for pension plans, 127
    for stock options, 132-33
Income taxation, influence of on
    accounting, 45-46
Institute of Internal Auditors, 161
Intangible resources
    discrimination in accounting for,
        149-51
    ignored in financial statements, 39
    in income determination, 147-48
    methods for valuation, 151-56
    uncertainty surrounding, 156-57
Interstate Commerce Commission,
    29, 30, 162
Inventory accounting; see also In-
    ventory valuation methods
    conflict between income and
        resource valuation, 64
    defined, 63
    "lower of cost or market," 72-73
Inventory valuation methods
    average cost, 68
    FIFO, 65-68, 70-73
    LIFO, 61, 68-73
        and income taxation, 69-70
    replacement costs, 70-72
    specific identification, 65

J

Jones, Ralph C., 35, 36

L

Leased fixed assets, 98-101
    and replacement value, 101

LIFO inventory valuation; *see* Inventory valuation methods
Liquidation and sale of business distinguished, 44
Livingston, J. A., 131-32

M

Management
  authority over accounting, 163-65
  compensation, 140-41
  relationship with corporation, 3, 13
Materiality, convention of, 41
Maximization of profits, 2, 20-21
Mergers, accounting for, 119-22
Merrill Foundation, 35
Minnesota Mining and Manufacturing Company, 142
Monetary concept of value; *see* Concepts of value and capital
Money, role of in accounting, 42-43
Moonitz, Maurice, 18, 35, 83, 167

N

National Association of Accountants, 161
Natural resources, 102-4

P

Pension plans
  accounting for, 124-31
  basic characteristics of, 125-28
  past service benefits, 126, 128-30
  tax aspects, 127
Permanence, convention of, 43, 55-56
Pooling of interests, accounting for, 120-22
Present worth as basis for asset valuation; *see* Concepts of value and capital
Price-level adjustments
  arguments for and against, 34-36
  procedures, 53-54
  relationship to replacement cost, 56-57, 71, 83
Productive-capacity concept of value; *see* Concepts of value and capital
Promotional expenditures, 63, 142-43; *see also* Intangible resources
Purchasing-power adjustments; *see* Price-level adjustments
Purchasing-power concept of value; *see* Concepts of value and capital

R

Replacement cost
  in accounting for
    fixed assets, 79-81
    inventories, 70-72
    natural resources, 102
  contrasted with adjusted historical cost, 56-58
  determination of, 54, 71, 79-83
  frequency of adjustment to, 71-72, 82-83
Research and development costs, 62, 142-43; *see also* Intangible resources

S

Securities and Exchange Commission, 162, 164, 165
Spacek, Leonard, 159, 160, 163, 166
Sprouse, Robert, 83
Stock options
  accounting for, 136-40
  annual income deductions, 138-39
  characteristics of, 132-33
  cost of, 133-36
  tax aspects, 132-33
Stockholders, declining influence of, 2, 12-13, 21, 107, 123
Straight-line depreciation, 87
Sum-of-years-digits depreciation, 90

T

Taxes; *see* Income taxation and accounting
Travelers' Insurance Co., 44

U

Uncertainty, reactions to, 156, 167-68
Uniform System of Accounts for Class I Railroads, 30
Uniformity in accounting, 26-33
  enforced, 29-31
United States Steel Corporation, 3, 34, 44, 60, 106
Unrealized income, 58, 72, 80, 104, 156
User depreciation methods, 88-89

V

Valuation of capital; *see* Concepts of value and capital
Valuation of resources; *see* Concepts of value and capital

This book has been set on the Linotype in 11 point Janson, leaded 2 points, and 10 point Janson, leaded 1 point. Chapter numbers are in 24 point Coronet Bold; chapter titles are in 18 point Caslon Lite. The size of the type page is 25 by 44 picas.